No Longer Bound

The Unborn Children

Tegra Little

Foreword by Theresa Burke, Ph.D

Noahs Ark Publishing Service
Beverly Hills, California

No Longer Bound: The Unborn Children

ISBN 978-1-7357447-1-1

Copyright © 2021 by Tegra Little

Published by:

Noahs Ark Publishing Service
8549 Wilshire Blvd., Suite 1442
Beverly Hills, CA 90211

www.noahsarkpublishing.com

Creative Input:	Laval W. Belle
Graphic Design:	Christopher C. White
Interior Design:	James Sparkman
Author Photo:	Shandon Youngclaus, Shandon Photography (Los Angeles, CA)
Front Cover:	Bronze statue by Jordi Jorda, Mundiart (Barcelona, Spain)

The subject, views, thoughts, opinions, and presentation of facts expressed in this publication are the author's own and do not necessarily reflect the views of the Publisher or its associates.

Printed in the United States of America © 2021 All rights reserved.
No part of this book may be reproduced or copied in any form without written permission from the author.

To my heavenly Father—the One who offers comfort to all.

To my husband Marc, thank you for your spiritual covering.

To my son Yakob, you are my gift and reward from God.

Contents

Foreword by Theresa Burke, Ph.D ix

Acknowledgements xv

Introduction 1

Chapter One
Do You Remember? 5

Chapter Two
It Happened Again 17

Chapter Three
The Awakening 31

Chapter Four
To Love and To Cherish 41

Chapter Five
Damaged Goods 55

Chapter Six
Trapped by Shame 63

Chapter Seven
Silent Sorrow 75

Chapter Eight
It Is Still Your Baby 95

Chapter Nine
Daddy Find Me | Apostle Paul 105

Chapter Ten
Purpose in the Pain 125

References 133

Contact 134

Foreword

Tegra Little is a woman of heart! The tenderness and strength of her heart's voice is expressed eloquently in the forthcoming pages of this book. She will lead you there gently and courageously, with love, compassion, and the lived authentic expression of her own story of loss and suffering.

The reassuring thing about grief is that the process cannot be tricked off its due course. It will forge its own path and take as long as it needs to carry you to its final destination. It is true that sometimes we might need to capture our grief and store it away for a time when we hope to feel stronger, or when a new situation in life gives us the stability and the security to allow the misty fog of tears to disrupt our vision without the fear of drowning in murky whirlpools. But if we are not attentive to its direction and prompting, a grief submerged will likely cost us more in the end.

One of the dismal elements of banishing feelings is that we fail to notice that our lives have become dangerously disconnected. Grief and heartache caused by pregnancy loss can take months or years to gather all the evidence and notice the details before you can understand the full impact of the loss. It's not unusual to entomb suffering as it turns into a great unfeeling numbness: a deadness inside. We no longer feel the sense of beauty and the privilege of being here as we lose sight of the invitation to thaw out the cold pieces in our shattered hearts that have driven out the fire of our deepest passions and sensitivity. As we lose faith in ourselves and learn to live in darkness, the heart will atrophy and wither.

Without a doubt, the state of one's heart shapes our lives in every human attachment and relationship. It's the place where everything is decided and given meaning, or discarded as disposable and an unnecessary burden, not worthy of our attention or care. Letting ourselves grieve by going directly into the pain, in manageable doses, is healing over time. Avoiding the pain ultimately forces it to be buried deep in the heart, where it subtly affects emotional, spiritual, and physical health. A fearful heart will avoid the blending of awareness by not giving oneself permission to feel, by guarding the dam which holds back a grief walled in darkness and denial. It's easy to forget the heart's moving thoughtfulness to everything that is happening to us. The heart absorbs the joy of things, but also its pain and grief. When you allow your heart to listen and be taught by what it carries, there is hope for transformation. Your burden will lighten, you will know that you are not alone, and that the darkness has served a purpose.

A courageous heart will take risks and move forward to connect deeply to oneself despite anxiety, pain, and confusion. A courageous heart will make space for the self to unite with its deepest pain with intention, to discover the truth and connect to the children who are invisibly bound to those emotions. A loving heart will awaken to its own spirit, the soul that longs to reconnect and remember as it engages with a heart unbound by grief to love. The power of your heart's attitude is revealed beautifully in the New Testament of MATTHEW 6:21. "*Where your treasure is, There your heart will also be.*" Because you see, whatever it is that becomes valuable to us will not only have our affection and love, but also our time, energy, and attention.

This book is a beautiful treasure precisely because it will lead you to your child as you acknowledge the irreplaceable life and the grief that comes from having relinquished little ones so intimately connected to your heart. Invoke the learning of every suffering you have endured because that child will lead you directly to the place where God dwells.

I was honored when Tegra invited me to contribute a foreword for this book. As the founder of Rachel's Vineyard Ministries, she and I are partners and soul sisters in ministry. Since 2012, her own organization No Longer Bound has offered Rachel's Vineyard retreats for those grieving the loss of a child. Her passion and ministry to others has grown out of her own journey of healing and that's the joy and sweetness of God's work in all of us. I am grateful for the seeds she has sown over many years in her special ministries for pregnancy loss.

As I facilitated Rachel's Vineyard all over the world, in scores of countries and even in other languages, I have seen the universal language of grief. As women, men, and grandparents shared their stories with a deep recognition of anguish, I repeatedly heard, "I've never told anyone." Although every person's story is unique, there are some common themes which stand out in what they shared. The first was an intense pain, a wrenching grief that was anchored by the depth of betrayal in what they had suffered. Many defined themselves because of what they were enduring. Others were shocked by the devastating and long-term fall-out of pregnancy loss, as it had risen and set upon the soul over a lifetime. The second theme was isolation. The word "secret" was uttered again and again, along with feelings of abandonment and shame. They might have been surrounded by people, it didn't matter. They felt isolated and fearful of sharing their secrets with anyone who might judge or invalidate their sadness. And third, the testimonies spoke of courage. Actually, hearing the incredible suffering that followed, and even the tumultuous acting out of mourning behaviors, revealed layers of despair and destruction. But the gift of remembering and mourning bears its fruit and harvest, because when the heart's grief is emptied there is room for a healing grace. This grace transcends the past, present, and future to fulfill the yearning for eternal peace, as the children are unbound. Remembered, reconnected, and reconciled, as you are received warmly at the burning hearth of your own soul with God, yourself, and the children.

You are holding courage and hope in the pages of this book. The act of reaching out for help, the act of breaking the silence that imprisons so many who have survived the trauma of abortion, miscarriage, or stillbirth is deeply authentic. It has led the author of this book into ministry and a mission to share the gift she has received. There is no time like the present to hold faithful to your heart. Gradually, you will come to find your way to friends who will open the doors toward new beginnings. So, let's launch the journey with Tegra Little as she uses her pain as a way to touch you, illuminating a path for you to remember the unborn children. Let silent tears flow, and when your eyes are clear, perhaps you will glimpse how your eternal child has been knocking at the door of your own heart. There is a treasure of blessing and love, like an unseen angel who will surprise your soul with a glimpse of heaven!

> *But now thus says the LORD... Do not fear, for I have redeemed you; I have called you by name, you are mine. When you pass through the waters, I will be with you; and through the rivers, they shall not overwhelm you...*
>
> ISAIAH 43:1-2

Theresa Burke, Ph.D
Founder of Rachel's Vineyard Ministries
Author of Forbidden Grief *and* The Unspoken Pain of Abortion

Acknowledgements

My Heavenly Father, thank you for loving me. I am confident that I will have eternal life with you through my Lord and Savior Jesus Christ. Thank you, Holy Spirit, for guiding my path every step of the way. This assignment would not have been possible without you.

Mom, your love and continual encouragement are never-ending and have blessed me more than you will ever know. Thank you for consistently modeling a servant's heart.

Paul (posthumously), thank you for sharing your story which allowed me to experience a level of emotional intimacy with you. I am forever grateful to God for his sovereignty.

Auntie Sharon, one of my cherished role models! Thank you for your love and relentless support.

Sis Charron, thank you for your prayers throughout my arduous journey. Your love and ongoing help are a blessing.

Sis Yolanda, I am proud of you for having the courage to parent.

Brother Brian (posthumously), thank you for always being there for me. I miss you and look forward to seeing you in eternity.

Cousin Sabina, thank you for your contagious love and willingness to make a difference where it counts.

Bishop Kenneth C. Ulmer, thank you for believing in the vision! You are a part of the fabric of the ministry and every life we touch. Lady Togetta "Tee" Ulmer, thank you for your steadfast support and prayers.

Laval Belle, and your team at Noahs Ark Publishing. God allowed our paths to cross ten years before knitting our hearts together for the book and other assignments yet to be revealed. Thank you for prodding and challenging me to enter into uncharted territory.

Sharon Hogg, before the foundation of the earth was formed God had a plan for our partnership. Thank you for your patience, insight, creativity, and heart of gold!

Charisse Bell, you are the epitome of a Titus 2 woman. Thank you for your wisdom, understanding, and discernment. God used you to help turn my mourning into dancing. I am forever grateful. I love you!

Dr. Theresa Burke, I am honored to partner with Rachel's Vineyard Ministries for healing after abortion. It has been one of the best decisions I've made in ministry. God has blessed you and your husband Kevin with an extraordinary gift. Thank you for equipping No Longer Bound Ministry to go forth and serve women and men deeply wounded by abortion.

Pastor Lucious Hicks, thank you for jumping onboard during the inception of the ministry. Your leadership was invaluable. Thank you for setting Marc up to pass the torch to him. To this day he's still scratching his head wondering how it all happened!

No Longer Bound family and leadership team, I cannot imagine working in God's vineyard without you. Thank you for your compassion towards others and for making your own wounds available as a source of healing: TeNita Ballard, Reverend Angela Brown, Marianne Castillo, Debbie Chandler, Jade Clarke, Dr. Lucien Cox, Charles DeCuir, Reverend Anthony Fields, Rodney Foster, Angela Franklin, Chloe Gitelson, Eleen Hupf, Reverend Shannon Jackson, Reverend Trecia Johnson, Dr. Roxanne Jordan, Pastor Marc Little, Dr. Linda Marcell, Reverend Tanis Matthews, Allison and David Medley, Terri O'Callaghan, Reverend Jacqueline Redeemer, Lisa Ridgeway, Sis Pat Roach, Elestine Smittick, Gloria Stoop, Linnie and Craig Weishaar, Sondra White, and Reverend Joyce Peters.

My gifted and anointed husband, Marc, thank you for your love, unwavering support, and guidance. Thank you for believing 1 CORINTHIANS 13:7 *"[Love] bears all things, believes all things, hopes all things, endures all things."* Our son, Yakob, thank you for being an exceptional gift and child of God. You can do all things through Jesus Christ who strengthens you!

Introduction

ONE DAY IN 2009, MY SOUL WAS AWAKENED BY THE following realization: *my unashamed brokenness is a far greater bridge to reach others than any superficial image of holiness.* The vision was crystal clear, and I could no longer allow the heavy weight of anxiety and fear to cripple me from walking in my divine, God-given purpose. I knew it was time to help others heal from the deep pain of abortion and miscarriage.

My uninformed decision to abort my child stemmed from the shame of getting pregnant out of wedlock. I was in college and knew I had a bright future ahead of me. Unfortunately, I did not have the fortitude to understand the consequences of sex outside of marriage. I opted to believe "it's just a blob of tissue, not a baby" which dehumanized my child. I selfishly destroyed a human life because I didn't want to be inconvenienced.

The only thing I wanted to do following my decision to abort was move forward with my life and forget what happened. This desire was short-lived, at least until the tsunami of emotions began to surface fifteen years later.

Abortion affects everyone differently, but all involved are touched in some way: mothers, fathers, siblings, grand-parents, aunts, uncles, nieces, nephews. It is a generational impact.

> *The most diabolical scheme of the 21st century, has been to convince a civilized society to dehumanize the most innocent human beings on the planet. Abortion is murder! It was murder when I encouraged several women to kill their babies because of my ignorant and selfish motives. The silence of the men who have abortion in their back-ground continues to feed the narrative that babies are not human. I encourage all men to extend their natural instinct to protect and provide for their families to include their unborn children.*
>
> DAVID MEDLEY

I can vividly remember the day my child was aborted. In fact, for many of us, if we allow ourselves to sit and meditate on our past experiences, God brings everything back to our remembrance. A man's role in abortion can take several different forms. He may have pressured you due to his unwillingness to become a father. Maybe he abandoned you, or drove you to the abortion clinic, or paid for the operation. It's possible you never told him you had an abortion until after the fact. Some men are naturally inclined towards providing for their children, and when that role is taken away, it can be devastating.

If you have experienced abortion or miscarriage you may develop the following symptoms:

- Guilt
- Grief
- Anger
- Anxiety
- Depression
- Suicidal thoughts
- Eating disorders
- Drug and alcohol abuse

The symptoms listed above are real. Some of us find ourselves suffering alone and in silence. Without help, the pain can linger forever.

No Longer Bound will help you see how abortion and miscarriage was detrimental to my overall well-being. I was stuck on a long and winding rollercoaster, waiting for the tumultuous ride to come to an end. The ride ultimately became a lot smoother but not until I was equipped with the right tools to help me along the way.

In 2009, I was called to ministry with the idea for my group, No Longer Bound, which was formed to help bring healing to women and men wounded from the pain of abortion and miscarriage.

Healing is a process, and one thing I know for certain is that time does not heal all wounds; time heals all wounds which are worked on.

Chapter One

Do You Remember?

AT THE START OF 2020 I ASKED THE LORD, "*WHAT are you doing in this new season. Is there a new vision to unveil? New plans to reveal?*" I sought answers to help me set things in place for 2021 and subsequent years. The God I serve is very strategic. He handles things on his time clock and within the seasons he chooses. A few months prior to year's end, a dear friend told me, "You have to pay attention to everything that's going on around you with sharp eagle eyes. Even if it's a stop sign, and someone is simply walking past, you must pay attention. I know it sounds crazy but kick up your senses!"

The reason for this conversation related to an interesting experience I had one day while I was getting gas. As the gas was being pumped, I went inside the store to get my son Yakob's favorite potato chips. He was seated behind me in his car seat. When I got back to the car, I handed him his chips and turned around to buckle myself in and start the car so we could depart. As I was turning the car key, I felt a tap on my right shoulder. The tap felt unusually different. I looked behind me and saw my son buckling his seat belt and getting ready to open his chip bag. I thought to myself, *"Did he touch me?"* I quickly asked Yakob, "Did you touch me?" and he said, "What?" I repeated my question, "Did you just tap me?" and he replied, "No, Mommy." It was bizarre to say the least. Nothing like that had ever happened to me before. I know it sounds crazy and rather out there because I thought the same thing. Well, quite perplexed, I paused for a moment and asked the Lord, *"Lord what are you trying to show me? Are you trying to get my attention?"* At that moment, a calm came over me. I closed my eyes and exhaled. I sensed He was letting me know it was time to get ready for something. There was symbolism with me putting on my seat belt. It was as if the Lord was saying, "Ready, set, go!" The time had come to accelerate! Hence, the aforementioned advice from my friend.

I responded by saying I would take her advice to heart and focus more to make sure I wouldn't miss what might seem like the smallest thing. By keeping this mindset, I believed God would sharpen his gift of discernment within me. I didn't want to miss anyone on my path for whom I could pray or share a word of encouragement. Not focusing on the smaller things in life could hinder a grand moment to encourage someone. Sometimes the smaller things are actually the bigger things.

Six little words: "Why don't you write a book?" A question posed to me by an intimate circle of friends over a ten-year period. They kept encouraging me to put pen to pad and start writing. I would look at them with a nervous little smile until I had no more excuses. This six-word question is one of the small things that gently nudged me to begin this storytelling journey.

Everyone who has had an abortion has a vital story. If they don't remember it, or only remember parts of it, hearing my story will often begin to trigger their memories during our No Longer Bound healing sessions. *"Oh my, she talked about when she first found out. She talked about her experience in the clinic, about the drive home with her mother. Did anyone ride in the car with me after my procedure? Tegra had her mother with her. What was the dialogue like between her and her mom? Her mom actually took her?"* There are different parts of my story that hopefully spark sharp memory recall. Based on years of ministry experience, I've found that women who have had abortions remember key parts of their story, but the rest remains in a very cloudy, gray area. Once they are in a room with other women, particularly in a group setting where everyone is telling their story, the Holy Spirit moves and begins to project images of what really happened. The subconscious relaxes and memories surface on the spot. I have heard hundreds of stories from women who have had multiple abortions. As they fill out their detailed application for No Longer Bound, some end up saying, "Well I *think* I had *x* number of abortions," only to realize as the questions probe deeper, the number increases.

One of our female leadership team members wrote a story one day admitting she thought she'd had five abortions but in actuality, had six. I knew early on she really did have six. During my one-on-one session with her, she kept repeating, "Tegra, I know I definitely only had five." I said, "Well I don't know. When I had a conversation with you two months ago, you thought you had six, then you said you were sure you had five." For two years this woman ran from the ministry. After she finally returned, the Lord began to uncover things in her life. She was ready to confront the truth. Her healing process was difficult and filled with turmoil, but during intimate time in prayer, she cried out to God and the Holy Spirit revealed she had indeed had six abortions.

In spite of the great challenges she faced confronting her past, there was another beautiful side to that struggle, as she received a revelation from the Lord. Months later during Thanksgiving dinner with her family, she realized six babies were missing from the dining room table. She confessed, "Tegra, for the first time ever on Thanksgiving Day I felt present, that I was really a mom for my kids that day." Previously she had a strained relationship with her kids. They told her, "Mom, we've never had a Thanksgiving like this. Everything is really beautiful. You seem different!" She was different because she was being healed.

During the first night of No Longer Bound's healing intensive group, God does something for both women and men. As I tell my story along with other ministry team leaders in small group breakout sessions, He activates the brain's memory. I trust that the Lord triggers their memories as they listen.

Someone asked me once why it was important to remember all of the abortions one has undergone. Why wasn't it enough to just know that they had them? My answer is, first and foremost, the Word of God tells us that we are fearfully and wonderfully made. He made us so intricately, everything about us is detailed. So detailed, that studies have shown when a woman is pregnant the cells from those children remain in her body after delivery. The scientific term for this is called microchimerism.

Evidence that cells travel from the developing foetus into the mother dates back to 1893, when the German pathologist Georg Schmorl found signs of these genetic remnants in women who had died of pregnancy-induced hypertensive disorder. Autopsies revealed 'giant' and 'very particular' cells in the lungs, which he theorized had been transported as foreign bodies, originating in the placenta. While Schmorl speculated that this sort of cellular transfer also took place during healthy pregnancies, it was not until more than a century later that researchers realized that these migrant cells, crossing from the foetus to the mother, could survive indefinitely.

Within weeks of conception, cells from both mother and foetus traffic back and forth across the placenta, resulting in one becoming a part of the other. During pregnancy, as much as 10 per cent of the free-floating DNA in the mother's bloodstream comes from the foetus, and while these numbers drop precipitously after birth, some cells remain. Children, in turn, carry a population of cells acquired from their mothers that can persist well into adulthood, and in the case of females might inform the health of their own offspring. And the foetus need not come to full term to leave its lasting imprint on the mother: a woman who had a miscarriage or terminated a pregnancy will still harbor foetal cells. With each successive conception, the mother's reservoir of foreign material grows deeper and more complex, with further opportunities to transfer cells from older siblings to younger children, or even across multiple generations."

ROWLAND, 2018 PAR. 3-4

Yes, these cells remain in a woman's body beyond her pregnancy and some never die. Have you ever wondered why women can sometimes be extremely attached to their aborted or miscarried child, to the point that they can't shake it? They try to detach but can't; mother and child remain biologically connected. We are truly fearfully and wonderfully created, more than we know.

The importance of remembering the number of abortions is critical. Plain and simple, every child is a life! Every child, created in the image of God, the *Imago Dei*, is a life and therefore important. How can we detach ourselves from that? We try and try, but ultimately, we can't. It is impossible. Even women in their seventies and eighties who have gone through our ministry devastatingly admit, "I just can't get rid of the pain, I need healing." Decades upon decades upon decades! I know those feelings intimately. I thought I could move on with my life after the abortion. I thought, "*Oh, I'm going right back to college and into my life like nothing ever happened.*" Not the case.

I knew something wasn't quite right when I first heard the word "abortion" eight years after I'd had one. I was at work, standing in a cluster of people that worked for me. We were in a hallway outside my office door. Nathan, a dear friend, was really excited because of a small ceremony one of his church pastors held for those who'd had abortions. Pastor Betty Williams was leading this particular service. He continued on to share a moment where Pastor Williams said, "If any of you have had an abortion, you need to release a balloon for that child." He may have even said they were to name the child. I looked at him like he had two heads because I couldn't believe someone would stand there and so openly share an unspeakable secret. I was mortified! The look on my face must have been one of panic. I'm pretty sure I did a quick about face back to my office. How in the world could he speak so openly about what was discussed in Betty Williams' group? That was the first time I heard the word "abortion" since I had aborted my child.

I quickly swept it under the carpet so I could go back to doing what I thought life was. But his words would not escape my mind. I kept thinking, *"How could he say that? How could he stand there and talk about abortion? Something must be wrong with me because he's free and I must not be free."* I couldn't even say to him, "Oh my gosh, you had an abortion too?" I couldn't share that moment with my friend. My shame had me imprisoned in that moment, keeping me from having a connection with him.

I could never tell anyone the secret of my abortion. Talking about it made me feel exposed and vulnerable. It was all in my head. No one else knew what was happening. I was so self-conscious and couldn't stop thinking, *"Oh, wait a minute, is someone looking at me? I better watch how my face looks right now because somebody may ask, 'Tegra are you okay?'"* I quickly said to Nathan, "Wow, that's deep, good for you." I had to get back to work quickly so I could stop myself from sinking.

That incident and other associated feelings blew away in the wind. The memory is vivid today. I wasn't haunted by that situation since I chose to suppress it, but it was all smoke and mirrors. I was moving up in management and my pain had to be buried in order for me to live. But I couldn't really live because I wasn't present with what I had done. My history with abortion was always there, screaming out but simultaneously suppressed. I shut the door in its ugly face immediately and those thoughts didn't return until many, many years later.

All the while, God was watching the whole thing. He is

so tender with us. He knew his daughter, Tegra whom he created, was not ready but she was going to get ready.

There are no accidents. I needed the sharp jolt of that circumstance to strike my conscience. Nathan and I worked together for many years. He is a mighty man of God. My husband Marc and I were close to him and his wife. I need to reach out to him to let him know what is happening with No Longer Bound. Even though he released a balloon that day, I believe he named his child. I'm not certain if it still gnaws at him. I want to thank him for being honest in the hallway during that time.

My Abortion Story

In 1984, I was seeing this guy for almost seven months. I was nineteen years old, in college, and heading into my sophomore year. He was good looking, intelligent, a little older, and seemed nice. We became sexually intimate, and I got pregnant. When I found out, I was afraid and couldn't tell him. Besides that, the shame of having to confess to my family that I was pregnant out of wedlock was more than frightening. Fear had me bound and the complete shame I felt was overwhelming. *"Here I am in college, with a good future ahead of me, and now I'm pregnant. Really?"* I panicked! The thought of the word "baby" never really settled with me. Some people explained it as a blob of tissue. My reasoning was, *"If it's just a blob of tissue, I need to get this blob of tissue out of me before it turns into a fetus."* That was my mentality. That's what I had to tell myself if I was going to get an abortion.

Two appointments were made at Planned Parenthood. The first was a consultation and the second was for the actual abortion procedure. I'll never forget my initial visit there talking with the office person. She counseled me, saying, "Well, you know you're still young and have your entire life. You can worry about kids later. You're in college and your focus needs to stay on your education." Her words definitely resonated with me. She was right, I needed to be in college. The office person told me I had to have someone bring me and take me home because I would not be able to drive afterward. I was thinking "*Who am I going to get to drive me? I can't tell anyone, and I can't drive myself home after the procedure.*" At this point I felt like I was going crazy because I knew I couldn't keep it all to myself. I didn't feel comfortable sharing it with my girlfriends either. At the end of the day the only one I could trust was my mother. I had to ask her to take me there and back. I was still living at home. I was raised in a Christian family. My mom is a believer. Her expression showed how sad she was to hear the news of my pregnancy and that I wanted an abortion. She didn't minister to me, she only said, "I'll take you Tegra, I'll take you." She was sorrowful. Looking back, it is really sad that I put my mother in the position of taking me to the death chamber for her grandchild.

My abortion procedure took place a few days after the consultation. I was approximately eight weeks along. My mother and I were so silent as we drove to the clinic, you could hear a pin drop. When we walked into Planned Parenthood the waiting room was empty. It was nice and quiet.

During the ultrasound, I asked the nurse to turn the screen so I could see the image of my baby. She snatched the screen, held it tightly and snapped back with a nasty, "No!" I remember it clearly. "Why not?" I asked. "We don't do that here!" was her mean, insensitive reply.

In my heart of hearts, I truly believe a way of escape was

provided for me in that incident. But because of the nurse's response, I blocked all thoughts of reversing my decision to abort from my mind. I should have put my clothes on, told my mom we were leaving, and run like lightning out of that clinic. But I didn't.

The walls in the procedure room were stark white, and the temperature was freezing cold. The doctor was a tall white man wearing a mask. He also wore a head covering that prevented me from seeing anything but his beady eyes.

I got on top of the table and the doctor told me to relax and that it wouldn't take long. He was right. It was over as soon as it started. The entire procedure seemed very quick, no more than ten minutes. I was absolutely numb and thinking to myself, *"Hurry up and get it done so I can put my clothes back on and get out of this place."*

After the procedure I went into the locker room area and found rows of post-abortive women. We all looked like zombies. I was mortified seeing them and wondered where all these women had been. They weren't in the waiting room when I walked into the clinic. Where did they come from? It was like a cattle call. We sat on the bench in front of our lockers and a woman came in offering us cookies and orange juice. The medication I was given prior to the procedure made me feel extremely lethargic, like I was drunk. I vividly remember saying, "Oh you all are so nice in here, you brought us juice and cookies." That was a lie. Nothing I experienced in there felt "nice." I felt like a zombie disconnected from myself. It was like an out-of-body experience.

I don't know how long I sat there before I was able to put my clothes on and walk back into the waiting room area to get my mom so we could leave, but I finally did. My mom stood up from her chair and looked at me. She put her hand on my back, we got in the car and didn't say anything. Not one word. I didn't have a conversation with her about everything that happened until 2006.

The morning after the abortion, no one was home, and the house was uniquely quiet. I had come to myself and what I'd done. I was in such a dark place and didn't want to get up. The weight of it all was excruciatingly heavy. While laying down in my bed the Holy Spirit entered my room and spoke to me saying, *"Get up."* I didn't get up because I was still in pain and bleeding, but I knew the Spirit of God was in that house. He paid no attention to my unwillingness to do his bidding. He literally picked me up, carried me into the living room, and placed me at the feet of Jesus. Lovingly He spoke, *"You need to repent and ask for forgiveness."* In that moment I pleaded, "Lord, I'm so sorry, I'm so sorry." After five minutes on my knees, my mind cleared. All that had happened completely vanished. I stood and walked myself back to bed knowing the Lord had forgiven me. Yet, I went right back to my old ways. I "returned to my vomit."

Chapter Two

It Happened Again

IT HAPPENED FIRST WITH WILLIE, MY STEPFATHER, and then again with the lifeguard at our neighborhood park. My stepfather molested me for the first time when I was five years old. One morning I awakened to find his hand in my underwear. It scared me to death! Was this a monster I was seeing or was I experiencing a nightmare? My body froze and my eyes bulged with horror as I thought, *"What are you doing to me? What is happening?"* The next morning, I woke up and got ready for school in the living room with my mother and siblings. While lotioning my legs I shared the previous night's ghastly experience, "I woke up and Daddy had his hands in my panties." My mom exclaimed, "What did you just say?!" I repeated what I'd said as my stepfather passed through the living room. He retorted, "She's a liar, she's just lying!" I ask you, what five-year-old makes up a story like that? As if it never happened, my mother never spoke of the incident again.

Willie molested me once between the ages of five and thirteen years old, but after I turned thirteen, the ugliness started again, and he darkened my bedroom with his unwelcome presence. Late at night he would come into the room I shared with one of my sisters. I was almost two years old when my mom married him. I was the only child with a different father but didn't know it at the time. For twelve years I thought Willie was my biological father.

I had a deep dislike, almost hatred, for my stepfather. In the back of my mind, without anyone's influence, I intuitively felt he was not my father. The gift of discernment was operating in my life at an early age. I knew something was off with this man. No one ever discussed this with me. My feelings were absolutely intuitive.

My Repulsive Stepfather

The molestation started again when I was thirteen years old and continued throughout the summer and during my eighth-grade year. He would come into the room and fondle my breasts. Every night I fell asleep in the fetal position with my arms crossed, protecting my chest and praying he would not turn my peaceful slumber into a haunting nightmare. I never said anything because he told me, "If you ever tell anybody I came in here and did this to you I will kill you." I was too afraid to tell, in case he made good on his threat.

My stepfather would come into my room late at night. I would jerk and push him away. I shared a room with one of my sisters, but she never woke up or knew that anything was going on. His abuse would only last for a few minutes, if that, then he'd walk out of the room. What man does this to a child? He was an absolute creep!

Outside of his nightly visits to my bedroom, we had no relationship. He never treated me like a daughter. All he did was drive us to school in the morning. The only positive thing I remember about him were the times we spent at family events. We had barbecue gatherings at the house and he made the best barbecue steaks, always tasty. Those were good times during the summer, with all the kids from the neighborhood and other family members playing. Other than that, I don't remember enjoying Willie's presence whatsoever.

I recall a very eerie incident with my stepfather when I was two years old. My family had gone to visit my Uncle Bill's house. Uncle Bill was Willie's brother. He and his girlfriend lived in a multi-level apartment complex and I remember running up to the top of the stairs. Willie grabbed me by the arms and started swinging me, like he was getting ready to throw me. He whispered, "I'm going to throw you down the stairs." I was so incredibly frightened thinking he was really going to do it. My mom shouted, "Willie put her down, put her down!" You could hear the stress in her voice. He put me down and said, "I wasn't going to throw her down the stairs." That was a lie. He was going to throw me down those stairs and make it appear to be an accident. This man was an evil, evil soul.

Another incident I vividly remember happened at the park. My immediate family on my mother's side, and some of Willie's side of the family were there. I may have been eleven years old. At the end of our time together we gathered everything up to put in the car and my mom left with some relatives. I was supposed to ride home with Willie and my siblings. I waited at the park for Willie to pick me up right where my mom told me to wait. He circled the park at least twice, literally looked right at me, and drove away. I know he saw me and left me there on purpose. I think he treated me this way because I wasn't his child. He also may have been jealous that I was the only one who had a different father. His molestation of me was his own perversion that served to hurt and damage me.

One day my mother came into my room to ask, "Are you okay? It seems like something is going on with you." In hindsight, what was going on with me was this molestation and abuse. But I felt like I didn't want to say anything to my mom, so I just told her that everything was fine. She said okay but I knew instinctively something was different. That was the only time she asked. Looking back, there were moments I walked around the house looking visibly sad, but she chose not to explore further after that first conversation.

During the summer when I was fourteen years old, I finally had the courage to tell my mom that Willie was molesting me. She was mortified. Without delay I was sent to live with my mom's younger sister, Aunt Carol, her husband, Uncle Fred, and their daughter, Cousin Deborah. I lived with them for probably three months or longer. During my absence, my mother was plotting her departure from Willie. Within months she filed for separation, followed by divorce. My mom's swift intervention protected me from further harm from my wayward stepfather. My mother finally divorced him just a few months after the separation.

The Negligent Lifeguard

When I was thirteen years old, some of the kids in my neighborhood and I enrolled in swimming lessons during the summer. My friends and I would walk to the park for fun time and swimming lessons. My mother and stepfather would pick us up some days, but most of the time, we would just walk to and from the park. We were a cluster of six or seven happy, innocent kids in our own young and carefree world, walking to the park for an afternoon of swimming.

Douglas, a handsome nineteen or twenty-year-old guy was the lifeguard and swim instructor at the pool throughout the summer. I remember telling my friend, cousin, and one of my sisters how cute I thought he was. Douglas would often single me out. Point blank, he was a predator and knew exactly what to say and do to catch me as his prey. One day, he invited me to the pool office and asked if I wanted to help file papers or help in the locker room. I said sure. One afternoon in the locker room, he started kissing me. It was shocking and my first real serious kiss. He stuck his tongue in my mouth, and I was shaken at how aggressive he was. At the same time, I was thinking, "*Wow he definitely likes me.*" As the days progressed, he brought me into the office to kiss me again. What I don't remember, and which remains a mystery to this day, is how I ended up at the park with him by myself. I was part of a group of six kids who went to the park together. One day I actually had sex with him, and my virginity was lost. I can't for the life of me remember how I was there without my circle. It's the strangest thing. Something in me still wants to drive over to that park to see if I can get into the room where it happened. I want to see if anything sparks my memory.

It happened in the back room, on top of a pile of sandbags where he'd spread a towel. Can you picture that? My first sexual experience, at age thirteen, on top of a stack of sandbags. We subsequently had sex several times. Next, he led me in conversations to see how I could come to his house. That was challenging and I didn't know how to make it happen. My mind became twisted. The enemy toyed with my thinking. I told Douglas I could create a permission slip, tell my mom I was going on a school outing, and the bus would pick me up at the park. I remember it quite clearly! How did I come up with fake trip slips? I didn't have access to a copy machine. Douglas must have orchestrated the process. I was able to get those slips to my mom and she gave me the green light to go saying, "Okay fine, no problem." How did I gain all this freedom? Who was watching me? Where was my protection, where was my oversight? It was nonexistent.

Those trip slips were how I was able to go to his house. One day, he asked me to bring some of my friends over to his house to hang out. I asked him, "What do you mean bring some of my friends?" He said, "Some of the friends you go swimming with." He was speaking of two of my dear friends, Constance and Simone. The three of us would always be at the park together, along with some of my siblings. I said, "Yeah, okay." I brought Simone and Constance to his house on one occasion. There was also another guy there, one of Douglas' friends. I remember his friend saying, "No man, I'm not doing this!" Constance said, "Tegra, Douglas is a grown man!" I defended him saying, "Oh no, he's a grown man but he's my boyfriend." Constance was no fool and struck me with, "You are crazy, he's a grown man and you should not be doing this." I was drowning and completely clueless.

The summer ended, and that was the end of it. The following summer he was working at a different park, and called to invite me and my friends to come by and swim. St. Andrews Park was located on Van Ness Avenue, a bit of a distance from my house. I went to that park and we joked and played around but nothing more happened. We continued talking throughout the years, he would check in with me to find out what was going on with me at school and so on.

I called him during my first summer at UCLA to let him know I was in college. He told me how proud he was of me. I was living in the dorms at the time, and he asked to pick me up for dinner. I told him that would be cool, so we got something to eat and ended up going to his house to just sit and talk about school. There was an awkward feeling between us, and we didn't sleep together. Now as I look back, I believe he didn't know how to respond to me as a young adult. He was uncomfortable. He was a pedophile.

That summer came to an end, as did my dorm experience. It was less expensive for me to be a commuter student. I was eighteen years old then, and returned to live with my mom who had remarried. One day Douglas showed up to the house and my mom came to my room to let me know that he was at the door asking for me. I was shocked. When I got to the door I asked him, "Would you like to come in, Douglas?" He said, "No, can you come out on the porch?" I said, "Yeah, what's wrong?" He asked me, "Is everything okay?" I said, "Everything is fine, why are you asking me if everything is okay?" He answered, "I just wanted to check to find out what's going with you, if you're okay." I told him that everything was fine, but I remember him looking extremely dejected, like something was going on. In hindsight, for some reason I think he may have caught a case. Maybe somebody else reported him. It's possible he could have been going around checking on girls that he molested to find out if they were involved in anything pertaining to reporting him. I am admittedly being very speculative here. That was the last time I talked with him. I never heard from him again.

Years later, something told me to look him up on Facebook. I found him, but his picture was distorted and blurry. I asked myself, *"why would he represent himself on his Facebook page with a blurry picture?"* I sent him a private message that said, "Hey Douglas it's Tegra, how are you?" He answered and said, "Oh my gosh it's good to see you, you look so beautiful, look at your pictures, what are you doing now?" I chose not to respond at all. Then something interesting happened in 2011. I started sharing my story with a male friend from No Longer Bound's leadership team about being molested by a lifeguard. I shared Douglas' name and he said, "Wait a minute, Tegra... what's his name?" I said, "His name is actually Creighton Douglas, but most people call him Douglas." He said, "I know him. He was a few years older than me. Creighton was always the type that everyone thought was so cool because he was good-looking and always running women. I always thought this guy was a bad seed even when I was a young teenager. I always saw him with different women and that's how I knew he wasn't a good guy."

I was also talking with another friend named Sam, a police officer who has since retired. I shared my story and he said, "Tegra, I know him." I said "What? You know him?" He said, "Oh yeah. He has cancer really bad. Let me pull him up on Facebook." By then I'd resigned from Facebook as I'd never been a big fan of social media. Sam said, "You can log into my account to view his page and check out the pictures." The last time we had communicated, he shared that he had a son who was about twenty-five or thirty years old. For a moment I had the strongest desire to tell his son what type of father he actually had. Then I scolded myself because I didn't know him or what kind of trouble and pain that would have caused. It was a fleeting thought that I immediately dismissed.

Douglas' Facebook pictures looked like death. He had an entire head of gray hair and he looked sick. I saw darkness in his eyes and thought to myself, "Wow, you are really messed up. You are still messed up." I was glad that Sam allowed me the opportunity. He said, "Tegra, I know some people that may be able to reach him. Do you want to talk to them?" I told him I'd actually like to have a conversation with Douglas and wanted his phone number. He said he'd see what he could do to make it happen. A few years have gone by, and Sam has not been able to locate him. My desire to reach out and talk to Douglas has slightly diminished.

A Time To Heal

In 2012, my healing began to awaken and stretch. Similar to someone laid comatose for years and finally wakes up. The joints are achy and pained and the muscles are tight because the body has been immobile, but the will to survive kicks in and the hard work it takes to overcome begins. My therapist helped me with many things but when my molestation stepped front and center, my grief found the space and freedom to express itself. As I came face to face with the truth, my healing began. My virtue was stolen by the very person who was supposed to protect me. He ended up abusing me.

One Sunday morning in 2012, a beautiful young pregnant

woman told a visiting pastor at the altar that she wanted to have an abortion. He asked her to remain right where she was, because he had someone he wanted her to talk to. The pastor found me in the sanctuary and brought us together for an introduction. She must have been nineteen or twenty years old at the time. She told me her story and I pleaded with her to not abort her baby. I let her know we had resources to help her. She was unable to control her tears. Understanding her pain, I just loved on her and prayed. I told her that God was going to send her an army of people who would walk alongside her. She would not have to walk alone. With heartfelt acknowledgement she responded, "Okay, okay, thank you, I'm so glad we met." I tell you God strategically ordered the right people to come alongside this young girl. We told her if she needed to move, we would finance it and help pay her rent. She would not want for anything. By any means necessary, we were going to save her baby's life. She ended up going to the clinic and having the abortion. I was devastated! Who does something like this when they are told they don't have to worry? Money wouldn't have been an issue. Nothing would have been an issue for her. Seven female ministers that God ordained rose to stand alongside this girl, but she aborted the baby. That threw me for a loop! We had mapped it out. Her mom and stepdad had threatened to kick her out and we said, "No problem!" We would help her find an apartment and carry the emotional burden.

At the beginning of 2012, I remember praying and asking the Lord to make me more compassionate. I wanted to make sure my level of compassion was deepened. This was the moment that challenged that compassion. When I found out this young girl had aborted her baby, I was thrown. To be perfectly honest, God was showing me this would happen many times, that this wouldn't be the last. God was stretching me, but because I was so dejected over what this girl had done, I felt I needed therapy to deal with it. Well, lo and behold, God is always up to something right? This particular circumstance is what got me into therapy. Little did I know He would use this experience to help me walk through the deeper waters related to my molestation and the seething hatred I had for my stepfather. During the months of therapy sessions, Willie was diagnosed with prostate cancer. I said to myself, *"You know what? I don't hate him. I feel sorry for him."* I found compassion for him. I didn't know what happened in his life to make him the man he was. That had nothing to do with me, but everything to do with him and the life he lived. Before he left this earth, I wanted him to know I forgave him for what he did to me.

I called my sister Charron, Willie's biological daughter who is two years younger than me. She still had something of a relationship with him, as did my brother Brian. My youngest sister Yolanda, on the other hand, wanted nothing to do with him. He never took care of them and didn't have a relationship with his grandchildren either. I said, "Charron, here is what I want to do. Why don't you just say, 'Daddy, we would all like to get together with you.'?" I said, "If you want to tell him that I will be there, you can do that, but you decide how you want to pose it to him." She said okay and decided to tell him. I asked her, "What do you think he is going to say? Do you think he'll say, 'okay I'll do it'?" She said, "I really don't know Tegra" He never followed up with her regarding that request. I tried to do my part and it was okay, my heart was in the right place. I had my peace. He passed away in 2016. I'm thankful my heart is no longer hardened toward him. God fixed it.

In January 2020, a group of team leaders from No Longer Bound decided to fly to Houston, TX to participate in the Grief to Grace retreat program. I remember praying *"Lord, what do you want to reveal to me on this retreat? I know I'm healed from the molestation, but I always know that a deeper work is available."* The Holy Spirit simply said, *"You'll see."* Throughout the five-day process, the revelation I received was that I needed to press charges against Douglas in spite of the statute of limitations and explore the next steps. I believe I wasn't the only girl he took advantage of. Maybe I could be a voice for the other voiceless women he used. I'm not sure if Douglas is alive today, but I should try to find out. When I shared with Sam that I was thinking about pressing charges he asked, "What do you have to lose?" I said, "I don't have anything to lose. Nothing!" Douglas had gone from park to park, taking advantage of young girls. What about the innocent girls and what he stole from them? What about the ones who haven't received any healing? Who knows what direction their lives took because of his behavior? Sometimes one single incident can change your life's direction forever.

For me, Creighton Douglas picked up and continued from where my stepfather left me. Two sick perverted men designed to ruin my life at an early age. The devil tried to destroy me at five years old, then returned to try again when I was thirteen.

My life was devalued at age five when I was touched inappropriately by my stepfather. It was also devalued at thirteen years old when I lost my virginity to a guy who was supposed to protect me. Deep down in my subconscious, I believe I carried the thought that if I didn't value my own life, how could I value the life of the child I was carrying in my womb?

I would say, out of the 400+ women who have gone through this ministry over the past ten or so years, 98% have experienced molestation. This current season we are looking at starting an abuse recovery arm of No Longer Bound. It will be a five-day retreat for men and women who have been physically or sexually abused.

Chapter Three

The Awakening

When I applied to colleges, I initially applied to the University of Southern California but wasn't accepted. I thought I wanted to be a journalist and applied to that department, but I would have had a better chance at being accepted if I had applied as undeclared, because USC's journalism department is extremely competitive. I was accepted at the University of California, Los Angeles and two other schools. I had a few friends at USC, and my aunt had also worked there. SC always lingered in the back of my mind while I was attending UCLA.

I met my husband Marc in the fall of 1985, when I was auditioning models for an on-campus show at USC that I was also helping to coordinate. In high school I had done fashion shows here and there, and always felt it would be great to work as a model to make some extra money. In my first or second year at UCLA I signed with Elite Modeling Agency. I was asked to come over to USC by a friend to help with their show. Marc was one of the models in the show and that's how we connected. We were both twenty years old when we met, eighteen months after the abortion.

There was nothing really special about my college life. I just wanted to hurry up and be done with it because of the stain of abortion. Closing that chapter so I could move onto the next one was my primary focus. I believed life after college would be much more fulfilling. In truth, I was running away from myself.

My first job out of college was as an inventory clerk. This position was my entry point into the largest record distribution company in the industry. Because I started working as a college intern, getting hired right after graduation was the perfect transition. I knew I was on a great path to having an exceptionally fulfilling career. I was in good graces with the company's management team and trusted that they were handling my career properly. My mentors were fantastic throughout my entire twelve-year stint in the record business, from intern to executive. What a great career! I have no regrets whatsoever. This work shaped me into who I am today, the talented mentors and executives I surrounded myself with contributed significantly to the success I found in my career.

Honestly, I wasn't sure what I was going to do for work at first. I initially thought I wanted to be a social worker. In my last year of college, I transitioned from being a junior at UCLA to a senior at USC. Panic was setting in because I needed to secure an internship. My thought process was that not having an internship meant not getting a job out of college. I knew a couple of people in the music industry who were highly successful background singers. After talking with them, I thought to inquire within the record business. I was in my early twenties, so I just opened the Yellow Pages and searched for every single record company I could think of. As a kid I would often see the RCA building on Sunset Boulevard off of Vine Street in Hollywood. I thought, *"You know, let me call RCA Records."* So I called them, and a woman named Lisa—who is still a friend of mine today—answered the phone. I said, "Hi, I'm a student at USC. I'm going to be graduating next year and would love to find out if you are looking for an intern." She sounded highly frazzled and replied, "Yeah, I need an intern, my intern just left, when can you get over here?" I could not believe what I was hearing! "What?" I started screaming because I was getting an internship! I could care less if it was only going to pay pennies, I just knew I needed an internship because of the potential for a position after graduation. Sure enough, we met, I interviewed with her, and started working the very next day. It was amazing!

I only spent a few months with her because the season was changing to summer and I didn't have any classes. I called at the end of summer and said, "Lisa, I'm going into my last year and I'd still love to intern with you. I'd really like to see if I could get something after I graduate." She answered, "Well I'm no longer at RCA Records. I'm at WEA Distribution working for Virgin Records and my office is out of WEA Distribution." Well of course, here I am, a novice who didn't know a thing about WEA Distribution. To top it off they were located all the way in Chatsworth. She told me she could possibly help me with gas and mileage for the commute and encouraged me that if I really wanted a job after graduation, WEA would be a good place for me and I would meet a lot of people. I accepted her offer and sure enough, doing so was one of the best decisions I ever made. That was where I was supposed to be planted. I ended up in an office with all the sales and radio promotional representatives that worked for various record labels that WEA distributed. I met many different people including executives and sales managers and made plenty of strong relationships. Following graduation, I was hired. I moved my way up the ladder to become the Vice President of Sales for Maverick Recording Company. It was an extraordinary twelve-year career!

The Wake-up Call

God was doing something towards the end of my career at Maverick. That's when I had a wake-up call. It was an epiphany, a revelation. I had a molar ectopic pregnancy in 1998. At that time, I had married my husband Marc and made the transition at Maverick from distribution to the label side. Finding out I was no longer pregnant and that a molar pregnancy is in the cancerous family was hard to digest. Ultimately, it all worked out. My tests proved I didn't have cancer, but my doctor wanted to make sure my pregnancy hormone count moved to zero. If it didn't, a major problem was imminent. Thank goodness it did ultimately move to the normal range. I had to have a dilation and curettage procedure, also known as a D&C. Right before going into surgery I told my OB-GYN that my husband didn't know about my abortion history and asked her not to reveal my secret to him. Looking back, I feel so bad about saying something like that to my doctor. I pulled someone else into my mess and that was not a good thing.

Several years after my surgery, my sister Charron said to me, "Tegra, I'll never forget how after your surgery Dr. Kelly came out to talk with us. She told us you had a lot of scar tissue. I had a quick thought in my mind, *'Oh my God did she have an abortion?'"* But at the time, my sister never said anything to me about it. The fact that I pulled my doctor into that mess, that I even told my mom to never say anything about the abortion, was selfish. I pulled other innocent people into my mess. Where was my mind? I was focused on the wrong thing.

After my first molar ectopic pregnancy in 1998, Marc and I weren't really trying to get pregnant again, but thought, if we did, great. Moving up the corporate ladder was always at the forefront of my mind, but it shouldn't have been my focus. My mind needed to be transformed to think about family first and not a career. I was wearing a serious blindfold.

Two years later in 2000, I had my first diagnosed miscarriage. There I was, looking at another pregnancy test and getting excited about it, and then a miscarriage occurred. Going to the doctor's office and hearing the words, "there is no heartbeat" is a burden I wouldn't wish on anyone, friend or foe. I was only eight weeks pregnant and completely devastated. I remember leaving the hospital and calling Marc to let him know what happened. My mind kept cycling through the thoughts, *"There is no heartbeat." "Maybe if I go back in two or three days, we'll find there was a glitch with the ultrasound."* I was trying to talk myself out of reality. I had a different OB-GYN this time who was wonderful. He confirmed, "No Tegra, you definitely had a miscarriage, and we are going to have to do a D&C on you." I thought, *"No way, this just can't be happening to me."*

All of my fertility challenges seemed to happen in the fall. My abortion was in March, so my child would have possibly been born in November or December. I was feeling very down during that time and Marc was in low spirits as well. I was still working at Maverick when all of this happened. One of the V.P.s pulled me into her office and said, "Tegra you may have to decide, think hard and long. Ask yourself, is this what you want to do? Do you want to have a career as an executive, or do you want to be a mom? How bad do you want to be a mom?" She was very genuinely sympathetic, tender, and supportive with me. Softly she said, "If you need to take some extra time off to sit with yourself and your grief, I'm all for that." I was so deeply appreciative. My direct boss felt the same way. They were all concerned about my well-being, which I really appreciated.

South Africa

My first trip to South Africa with Marc in September 2000 was very significant. Marc had already visited the country twice on business. On our second or third day there, we visited one of the shanty towns. I couldn't believe the depth of poverty I witnessed for the first time in my life. It was truly shocking to see what I saw post-apartheid. We walked by shacks made of corrugated metal that appeared so fragile that one could take a baseball bat and knock them all down. But one woman, a ray of sunshine, came out of her tiny house which was no larger than my bedroom. She wore the most beautiful smile and invited us into her home. All she wanted to do is show us where she lived. She was a woman of God and filled with much joy. She talked about God and though she didn't speak English well, she could say the word God and you could feel the essence of her sentiments. Her happiness was unforgettable, and her eyes glistened. Her love was palpable. I said to myself, *"Oh my gosh God, what are you doing?"*

I was transformed in South Africa. Walking out of her tiny home, we walked a few more steps to a school close by. Many children came out and sang to us. They were happy, vibrant, beautiful, and innocent. I loved what I was witnessing, and in that moment, I thought, *"What am I doing with my life? Yes, I have this amazing job and an exciting career, but it doesn't mean anything. Yes, I have a six-figure salary, but so what? Here is a woman with little or nothing, and she had unspeakable joy with the bare necessities of life. I am working ten-hour days, flying around the country, I'm tired as all get out! I need to be a better wife. I need to be a mother. Am I not getting pregnant because I am stressed out? What am I doing with my life?"* I began to pray. Marc had no clue what I was doing. I began to ask the Lord to give me a way out of working in this rat race of an industry. I was ready to get out of that business.

These feelings didn't connect with me until I stepped onto South African soil. My eyes began seeing things differently. I had a new vision and found myself longing for something I didn't have, something that felt truly significant for the first time in my life. I no longer cared about business or moving up the ladder. My career took a back seat as it became meaningless in comparison to what I was experiencing. What I was desiring for my life became meaningful. I wanted to live in purpose. All that other stuff was not purposeful for me. My perspective began to shift.

I left the industry in 2001. When I returned from South Africa, I began fervently praying, *"Lord give me a way out!"* I felt like I needed to begin putting things in order so that just in case the door opened, I could leave without any problems. I wanted to make sure the people who worked under me could remain employed without me, because the Lord was showing me there were bigger and better things for me.

One day my boss, who I loved immensely, called me into his office and said, "Tegra, it looks like there will be a few departments folding into Warner Bros." My department was one of them. He had planted a seed at the end of 2000. The record label was no longer doing well and there was a possibility some of the departments were going to be absorbed by Warner Bros. My boss didn't know what was going to happen, but he wanted me to be aware that there was a possibility of it happening. That was the best news I could have received. I had an executive contract, so it didn't really matter to me if my department was going to fold. On paper I still had fifteen months left. In March of 2001, he said, "Tegra, it's quite probable the sales department is going to fold into Warner Bros. in the next two to three months." I was super excited, because I knew all I needed to do was make sure the people in my department were taken care of. I did have to let one go, but there was one young lady I wanted to make sure was planted elsewhere within the company. Sure enough, I was able to take care of her. All of the paperwork in my department was handled, my i's were dotted and t's crossed. Everything was decent and in order.

The day my boss informed me of my last day in the department, I felt like I had pom-poms in my hands. I was on a mission to make sure every little thing was taken care of. The books were correct, so I could leave with a clear conscience. In June 2001 I was able to walk away, and I never looked back. That was the end of my career. I had a great interview with another distribution company, which I really thought I wanted to work for. I was having lunch with the president and he said, "You know Tegra, we can really use you over here." They were probably going to pay me over $200,000 a year which at that time was a lot of money. I felt like the enemy was dangling a carrot in front of my face. I said to myself, "*You know what, I'm done.*" I didn't know what God was going to do, but I was done. I had a year and three months left on my contract, so I was still going to get paid. I never looked back and the rest is history.

Now to put things into perspective. During the summer, an event was put on at Faithful Central Bible Church and Marc was speaking during the event. At the evening service, he called me up onto the pulpit and laid hands and prayed over me. He said, "You think you're coming out of the workforce to be a mom, but you are coming out of the workforce to do ministry." His words flew so far over my head, I didn't know what he was even talking about. My friends who were in attendance also didn't know what he meant. In unison we all said, "What! What?" My mind was swirling with thoughts, "*How farfetched! What does he think he is saying! This is crazy! He shouldn't have said that in front of all these people!*" Well, he was right! No Longer Bound was birthed before I became a mom. Then we adopted.

Chapter Four

To Love and To Cherish

MY HUSBAND MARC WAS ALREADY SAVED WHEN we met. I had accepted Christ when I was nine years old, and I think he accepted Christ when he was probably twelve. We are only months apart in age, both born in 1965. We were saved with one foot in the world and one foot in the church.

He didn't know about my abortion prior to our marriage. Marc graduated from USC in May of 1987, while I was still attending UCLA. In July of that year, he was shot by a gang member and I witnessed the entire incident.

At a strip mall near USC's campus there were off-campus apartments. On the first floor of that building were lower-level apartments with a door that opens directly onto the street. During this time, Marc and I worked at Continental Airlines as college students. That is how we were able to travel all over the world. One night, I came back to his apartment after work. He was the only one living there at the time, because he had already graduated from USC and his roommates had left for the summer. I got into the apartment and wondered where he could be. I knew he had a major accident in Palm Springs the weekend prior when he ran through a sliding glass window that appeared to be open. The glass was so clean it looked like an open door. He ran through the glass and cut his feet bad. I knew he couldn't have gone far on foot because of this injury, and I had borrowed his car while mine was in the shop. I waited for him in the apartment, looking out the window all the while.

Before I saw Marc, these two guys pulled up in front of his apartment building in a car that seemed to be having mechanical trouble. The driver got out of the car while the passenger stayed inside. The driver started to bend one of the windshield wipers, which seemed crazy to me. I was able to really observe these two for at least fifteen minutes. The passenger asked the driver what he was doing, and he replied something like, "I'm just trying to take care of this, don't worry about it." Finally, I saw Marc crossing the street toward the apartment. He was coming from the 32nd Street Market, he had just gone across the street to get some bread. I ran to open the door leading to the street and as soon as he reached the sidewalk, I met him. The driver of the car beckoned to Marc saying, "Man, can you help me fix this?" Marc answered, "Fix what?" I said, "No, no, do not go over there. I've been watching these guys and something's not right with them." Marc was a naïve guy from Connecticut. Just because these guys asked for help didn't mean he needed to help them. Marc moved a little closer and said again, "Fix what?" The driver shouted, "Fix this!", and pulled out a 12-gauge shotgun. Marc and I began freaking out as we both backed up onto the grassy area outside of the apartment. The guy continued on, saying, "You better give me at least $100!" Marc said, "Man, I don't have any money!" He dropped his bags and emptied his pockets and pleaded, "I don't have anything!" Coins began falling out of his pocket as the driver yelled, "Don't lie! Don't lie to me!" He lifted his gun and hit Marc on the left side of his shoulder and head area. I ran back into the building as he lifted his gun and knelt down because Marc had fallen to the ground. The guy cocked the gun and shot Marc in his upper right leg. The shooter raced back to his car and drove off and I immediately ran back outside. Marc cried out, "Just go get help, Tegra! Go get help!" He didn't have a phone inside the apartment, and there were no cell phones at the time. I looked upstairs at some people on the next level, and started screaming, "Call the police, call the police, there's been a shooting here!" The police arrived instantly. The medics weren't sure he was going to make it. There was so much blood, and his head was hydrocephalic. When I saw him in the ICU his head had enlarged three to four times its natural size and his body was swollen. It was dreadful.

My mom and my brother Brian ran to my side at the apartment building as Marc was being placed inside the ambulance. I felt like a crazy person having an out-of-body experience. I was telling my mom that the angels had been there to protect me because I didn't get shot. My mom encouraged me to calm down and just breathe. When we got to the hospital that night, my brother stayed with me and my mom ended up leaving. I clutched a bible that was in the waiting room to my chest and rocked back and forth as I sat there, freezing cold. My brother, who was only nineteen years old at the time, kept a steady eye on me. He was concerned. I was experiencing PTSD, breathing heavily and rocking with that bible clutched to my chest. Weeks later, Marc had to have his entire right leg amputated. Because he was shot with a 12-gauge shot gun, all of the pellets ravaged his skin when the bullet entered his body. He ended up getting gangrene in his leg, and his foot was swollen, green, red, and black. I kept saying his foot was going to be taken, with no idea his entire leg would be amputated.

We hadn't been dating that long. This was in July 1987, and we'd met each other in October 1986. We didn't officially start dating until December or January after we met. My family said, "If you don't really love him, now is the time to step away." I was a bit stunned, thinking, "*What? Who has a conversation like this? What do you mean, step away? Look what has happened to him.*" Others were saying, "Tegra isn't going to stay with him. She's not going to deal with an amputee, she's not going to stay." I said, "I am going to stay because he is a great guy." It would have been easy to leave, but I really loved him. He had the surgery for his leg to be amputated at the beginning of August, then went into rehab for four or five months and was fitted for a prosthetic leg. Living with Marc as an amputee was never an issue. He was still the same great guy. The only difference was he did not have a leg, so he walked with a cane and a limp. That's it.

When he was going through rehab, we had a few counseling sessions together with a gifted Christian counselor. We sat with her for several sessions, and she kept wanting to talk about the amputation. The amputation wasn't the issue at all. The issue was that he thought I was cheating and lying about it. That was the center of attention through pretty much all of our counseling sessions. But the therapist was looking at us like, "So you guys don't have a problem with the amputation?" We replied, "No we don't." She was perplexed and wore the most incredulous look on her face.

Spiritual Gifts

When I came to learn more about spiritual gifts, I knew God had given me the gift of discernment. This gift was at work the moment I knew something wasn't right the night Marc got shot. I love the way we are created. When we are in tune with our spiritual gifts, we cannot walk away from them.

The gift of discernment is real. If Marc had listened to me, and not walked up to the car to help that guy, he would still have his leg. I'm always considerably sensitive to my surroundings. Because of the trauma I suffered during the shooting, my discernment is heightened. Even at nineteen years old in that abortion clinic when the woman told me I couldn't look at the ultrasound of my baby, I had the feeling that I should have escaped. I believe that was my way out. I should have put my clothes on, run into the lobby, and said, "Mom, let's go." Out of fear, I chose to squash it.

I dated Marc for a long time. He was ready for marriage much sooner than I was. We finally decided to be celibate and abstain until marriage. I had just graduated from USC and wasn't sure about the direction I should go. He was thinking about getting an MBA, and then thought about going to law school. I was a little all over the place and needed to figure out what I was going to do with my life. It all stems from the lack of meaningful discipleship. My step-grandmother was the one who really tried to disciple me, but my mindset was so completely worldly. I know hindsight is 20/20, which is why now when I disciple women, particularly women on the verge of getting married or dating someone seriously, I ask, "Why are you waiting? Go ahead and get married. Grow together! Even at twenty-three or twenty-four years old, you can still grow together, don't wait." They say things like, "Oh no, I'm waiting to see what he's going to do with his career." My response is usually, "Why? You are Christians! You believe in the Lord and He has a plan and purpose for your life. Begin premarital counseling with a well-qualified counselor. Make sure your mate has been properly vetted by people you trust, love, and who have your best interest at heart. Why wait?" I say my mindset was worldly because I was focused on how I was going to make money. Marc was a man made in God's image! He had a hope and a future for him. Marc ended up going to law school and passing the bar on the first try. As a matter of fact, he ended up taking the bar a few months before we got married. He was hoping and praying he would pass the first time so he could enjoy the early days of our marriage without the stress of having to study. But we dated for eight or nine years before we got married. We waited far too long all because of me.

After my awakening in South Africa, God answered my prayer. He gave me a way out of the entertainment rat race, and I was no longer tied to the money. My desire was for a deeper relationship with the Lord, to be a better wife, and to become a mother. God had opened the door to allow all of these things to happen and I knew He had a plan for my future.

We had a long, tumultuous journey trying to start a family with children because of the molar ectopic pregnancy followed by the miscarriage. I had a second molar pregnancy in December 2003, followed by a partial hysterectomy in July

2004. In October 2004 I was diagnosed as cancer free which was purely a blessing! During the month of October, the Holy Spirit spoke to me saying, *"I am taking you into a season of loneliness."* I lived with depression the entire year of 2005. For the first time, I began to grieve the loss of my aborted child. The depression came from my grieving the loss of my womb and not being able to carry a child. No one else knew but me. I still had my ovaries and Marc's sperm, so we chose to go down the path of gestational surrogacy. We agreed to have someone else carry our child.

In the back of my mind, I was thinking Marc needed to be with someone else. I was really pushing him away in a way because of my own depression and inner turmoil. Looking back, I believe my identity was wrapped up in my ability to have or not have a baby. I even questioned myself, *"Am I less than a woman because I can't bear children? My husband's child? Gosh, we shouldn't even be together. He should be with someone who could carry a child for him."* The enemy took residence in my mind with accusations in tow, and Marc didn't know I was suffering.

At the beginning of 2006, we experienced major marital problems. For Christmas 2004 Marc bought me a ten-carat yellow diamond ring. He always said he wanted to give me this gift when I birthed his first child. I lost it in January of 2006. It was in my pocket while I was working on creating high-end custom invitations for a client. I placed it in my pocket while I was running errands and lost the ring. He was enraged to say the least. The ring was not insured because the cost to do so was rather exorbitant. I had the attitude that I couldn't believe it wasn't insured and actually thought it was. There was a big divide. He told me I was careless with the ring just like I had been careless in our relationship. That statement was indicative of what was happening throughout 2005. I was depressed and mentally absent. I was going through a lot, silently and alone.

Time to Break the Silence

I began praying after I lost the ring because I knew we were in trouble and didn't know where our marriage was going. At the same time, I thought, *"Well gosh, it's a material thing. Can a material thing divide us? Can a material thing lead us down the road to divorce?"* It didn't seem possible but first and foremost, it didn't seem godly. The Lord spoke to me and said, *"You need to get some help because you have not accepted my forgiveness for the abortion."* That was a light bulb moment! That is why I was depressed in 2005, and at the top of 2006 I'm hit with having serious problems within my marriage. I had to figure things out and asked the Lord to help me find a therapist. I was suffering and didn't know what to do. A great therapist did come my way, thank God.

I was never suicidal but remember feeling sad continually. It felt like I'd been kicked in my stomach and was gasping for air at every step. Thinking about it now brings tears to my eyes. I clearly remember calling a girlfriend of mine at the time while I was driving. I was sobbing so hard and sharing what was going on in my marriage, how I needed prayer, and what had happened with the ring. She told me to just leave it at the altar. I thought, *"What in the heck did she just say to me?"* I was utterly appalled! She placed a band-aid on a gaping wound. I felt like screaming through the phone, but the Holy Spirit told me he would send me new people with hearts of empathy who I could really talk to. People can only give you what they have. That is all my friend had, but it hurt so much because I was in such a dark place. I was crying out and needed a deeper level of ministry. In that moment the Holy Spirit was telling me to pump the brakes and end the conversation. An anointed therapist came into my life and I saw her for two months, about once or twice a week. Toward the end of our time together, my healing was definitely fast approaching. She asked me if I was thinking about talking to my mom. I told her yes, I wanted to. Then she asked if I'd thought about talking to Marc and I told her no. I didn't know if I could do that. She suggested I start with my mom.

I called my mother and told her I really wanted to talk to her, and she came over to the house. This was the first time I had ever talked to her regarding my feelings about the abortion. First and foremost, I apologized to her for murdering her grandchild. She knew we would one day have this conversation but was waiting for me to bring it up. She said, "I didn't think it was something I should do." My mom and I were bawling at the dining room table. I told her I was getting counseling about what happened, and about Marc and I having problems. I said, "I need to tell him, but I'm scared to tell him about my past." Mom encouraged me and said, "I'm praying, and you don't need to worry about anything when you share with Marc." I said, "Mom I'm owning what I did and don't blame you, but I do have questions. Why didn't you stop me? Why didn't you minister to me and stop me from doing what I had set out to do?" She answered, "Tegra you asked me for help. You asked me to take you to the clinic and I did the best I could for you by telling you I would take you." I said, "I understand, Mom." She went on to say, "Was that the best decision? No, but I thought I was just being there for you and helping you do something that you asked me to do." I accepted her answers and thought it was a great time of healing for both of us. We needed to have the conversation. That topic was closed with my mom and took place about one month after my last counseling session. Two months later, I called my therapist and told her I'd been praying and felt it was time to talk to Marc. She encouraged me and assured me all would be fine. I'll never forget that day. I called him on the phone and told him I needed to talk to him when he came home that night. He could tell I was really nervous about whatever it was and said, "Are you alright?" I said, "I just need to talk to you when you come home." I was wringing and squeezing my hands while I was talking with him. I was so nervous that I was shaking, he could probably hear it in my voice.

It was mid-afternoon. I remember the sun was on the west side of the house, shining through the French doors that lead into the living room. The sunlight was piercing through the living room. When Marc arrived home, he came down the stairs. I was sitting in the living room and he asked me what was going on. When he sat down, I said, "I really need to talk to you, but I'm extremely nervous to tell you what I need to tell you." He said "Tegra, what is happening?" I just kept sitting there across from his chair in the living room, staring at him and not saying anything for a good five minutes. He asked again what was wrong. I got down on my knees and crawled to where he was sitting and said, "I don't know how to tell you." He said, "Go on I'm here, I'm listening." I kept breathing deeply and sighing at the same time because I was bound. Feeling like I had a pile of bricks on my shoulders I said, "I want you to know that before I met you, I had an abortion at nineteen years old. I never told you the secret. After the counseling I've been doing over the last couple of months, I felt like I'm supposed to tell you what happened with me. I told my mom I was deeply sorry for murdering her grandchild, but I am so sorry I took this secret into our marriage. This was before I met you. I was afraid to tell you."

I really started feeling like the Lord was punishing me. To have a partial hysterectomy and not being able to carry a child ever again was my punishment. Hence, the Lord told me I needed to get help. I hadn't fully accepted his forgiveness, and there were consequences to the bad choices I made. Reality had set in. When I talked to Marc, I also told him I was depressed throughout 2005, and how the Holy Spirit had spoken to me in the fall of 2004. He was going to take me into a season of loneliness. I shared every detail with him. Looking into his eyes, I was drowning in my tears. I apologized for keeping the secret and for all my infertility problems. My husband stopped me, laid hands on me and started praying over me like he had never prayed over me before. He could see the spirit and spoke with such authority, breaking the shame, condemnation, and the spirit of abortion. We then embraced and he said, "I am sorry you experienced that. I am sorry you've been carrying this weight. I'm just sorry." It was a beautiful tender moment. A really powerful moment. I called my therapist and told her what happened, she's a deeply spiritual woman and said I was going to be just fine. A few weeks later she called and said, "Tegra, you know I'm doing some work over at City of Refuge Church with some young women and I would love for you to come and talk to them about your abortion and testimony." I swiftly said no, I could not do that. As soon as the words left my mouth, I knew I was still bound. I asked myself, *"Am I not healed? Oh, how could I say no after God had done all of this in my life these last couple of months. How could I say no to this request?"* I was still stuck, but it was okay because God planted the seed that day my therapist made her request.

Launch of No Longer Bound

Two years later, in 2008, I was praying and asking the Lord what I could do in ministry. I started discipling fifteen or so women with my dear friend Valerie. We created a detailed intake questionnaire with a lot of questions about sexual abuse and abortion. Three out of the fifteen ladies at that particular time had abortion in their background. I started seeing all these different symptoms manifesting before my eyes. Anger, rage, depression, mood swings, guilt and grief, all of it! I was intrigued and found the things that were happening with these women so interesting. In 2006, the Lord had planted those seeds with my therapist's request.

Backing up for a moment, after my therapist asked me to go to the City of Refuge and I didn't go, the Holy Spirit said, *"I want you to start a ministry for women who are hurting from the pain of abortion."* I said, *"No."* I look back now and see how early God had planted that seed. The women graduated from the program a little over a year later, in the summer of 2009. After they graduated, I started praying and asking the Lord how he wanted to use me in ministry. I knew he wanted me in ministry but didn't think I was supposed to have a discipleship group like that. The Lord spoke to me and said, *"You already know, Tegra."* That's when he downloaded the vision and allowed me to see No Longer Bound. I believe I was at the dining room table when the Lord gave me the scripture,

LUKE 4:18 (NKJV), *"The Spirit of the Lord is upon Me, because He has anointed Me to preach the gospel to the poor; He has sent Me to heal the brokenhearted, to proclaim liberty to the captives And recovery of sight to the blind, To set at liberty those who are oppressed; to proclaim the acceptable year of the Lord."* I couldn't believe what was happening to me, because I was getting clarity about what He wanted. Again, He spoke to me saying, *"You already know, you don't even have to think about it."* He gave me the ministry name right in that moment, "No Longer Bound." I didn't know how to put this Kingdom Revelation together. In hindsight, what Valerie and I did in the discipleship group with those young ladies created my blueprint. I already knew how everything should be worded for the ministry. There needed to be some sort of package I could send to Bishop Ulmer and I needed to talk to him. In my mind, I kept thinking he was not going to allow me to have an abortion recovery ministry out of my home church. I was sure he would say no.

He gave me the foundational scripture, the name of the ministry, and the details for what the ministry should look like. When I sat down with Bishop Ulmer in September of 2009 and gave him the vision I said, "Bishop, God has given me a calling." I began sharing my back story and said, "I know this is my call, beyond a shadow of a doubt." He just sat there and looked at me. We were at Kate Mantilini's in Beverly Hills for lunch when I shared the vision the Lord had given me. He said, "Tegra, we are going to do this." I said, "We are?" He answered back, "Yes we are going to do it." I felt like a kid in a candy store. "Yes!" We launched No Longer Bound in January of 2010 and the rest is history.

Chapter Five

Damaged Goods

THOUGH I WASN'T COGNIZANT OF IT, I WAS A POSTER child for damaged goods. Immediately following my abortion, I disconnected from the whole ordeal. Looking back, it is clear to see I was only concerned about outward appearances. *"Let me continue to climb the executive ladder in the record business. Let me manage my staff well. Let me be elevated in the eyes of the entire management team. If I'm successful, no one would ever think I had an abortion."* Climbing to dizzying heights of success in business was my entire focus, it meant everything to me. I was a college intern getting ready to graduate knowing I was in great standing at the number one distribution label in the business. I defined myself by a career which supposedly fed my self-worth. Instead of identifying myself by who I was in Christ, my worldly mindset greenlit the construction of a lie. People around me affirmed my behavior rather than pull me aside to say, *"Hey, who does God say you are? You are a Christian."* Well, I was not discipled as a young person and didn't allow myself to be discipled until I was thirty-six years old.

After leaving Maverick in 2001, one of my friends invited me to attend an intimate discipleship group led by a wonderful mentor, Minister Traci Shelling. Minister Traci asked a few who were already a part of the group to reach out to other women who might be a good fit. The timing for me was impeccable, so of course I gave a resounding "Yes!" This was exactly what I needed.

Our group met once a week and we were assigned prayer partners, something quite new for me. Previously I only prayed on my own, or occasionally with friends, but never on a weekly basis. I loved it, but what I loved more than anything was the sisterhood I found with the other women. We were a tight-knit group and truly there for each other in the trenches. The group was a safe, sacred space where we opened up about our lives, our connection was woven with trust that fastened our hearts together. Minister Traci didn't allow us to linger too long though. When the Lord showed her time was up, she knew she had to push us out of the nest to fly on our own.

Interestingly enough, even in the small close group, I did not talk about my abortion. These women were there for me when I had the second molar pregnancy, partial hysterectomy, and throughout my depression. Yet, I said nothing about the abortion until I was ready to walk in the calling God had given me for No Longer Bound. That's when I told them what God said. The discipleship group was a huge part of my spiritual growth, it was the place I learned how to press into the Lord and study his word. We prayed once a week at six in the morning, and I grew exponentially in a deeper and more meaningful relationship with Him. I made a dedicated prayer closet soon after I started praying with these women.

The anointing was consistently heavy within the group. I had never really been in an intimate atmosphere with women who had such a powerful prayer language. One morning while in my prayer closet, I implored the Lord saying, *"Lord will you please just rain down my spiritual language. Rain down, bless me, hit me with my heavenly language."* As the old saying goes, be careful what you ask for, you might just get it. The Holy Spirit fell on me and I was completely astonished. My house has four levels, and my prayer closet is at the very bottom. The master bedroom is situated right above the closet so I thought, *"Marc must be hearing me right now. What am I saying? What is this?"* I was deep in the spirit and felt I'd been caught up for an hour. I ran out of the closet and upstairs to Marc. "Babe!" He asked, "Are you okay?" I responded, "Could you hear me? The Holy Spirit fell on me and I was praying in tongues!" He sat straight up in bed and said, "Are you serious?" I said, "Yes! I've been silently praying but never said anything to you about it." He answered, "Oh I didn't know that, but I did not hear you." It was 6:30 a.m., and I called Minister Traci to share my news of being filled with the Holy Spirit and speaking in tongues for the first time. She was excited for me and said, "It's powerful, Tegra. God has something for you with that gift!" Boy, she was spot on!

I was still hiding my deep, dark secret. My career obscured the cloud constantly hanging over my head. The funny thing is, anyone intuitive—or shall I say, spiritually gifted—could look at me and say, "You know what, something is wrong with her." This was before I started with my prayer circle. I have a ninety-year-old step-grandmother named Barbara who is still alive today. Marc and I had a weekly Bible study with her prior to getting married. Marc was really seeking God for wisdom and wanted to do things right, including for us to stop fornicating. Barbara definitely spoke into our lives. She asked if we called ourselves Christians and our answer was affirmative. She told us, "Well you need to act like it, and stop behaving like you are a part of the world." When we were going through that process with her, she used to look at me as if she saw right through me. My, she was a very discerning woman with a piercing gaze. In hindsight, she may have seen something in the spirit, but never said what she saw.

When you think of damaged goods, you might visualize a bent can you brought back from the grocery store. The way it was sitting on the shelf hid the dent, but when it gets home and is removed from the bag, there you see and feel it, clear as day. Or you may think about an irregular dress on the sales rack. It looks good on the hanger, but when it's tried on, something just doesn't feel right.

I've always been very open, conversational, and engaging toward others, but looking back now, after the abortion, I did not exhibit these qualities. I was somewhat reserved and standoffish. But working in entertainment, being extremely sociable was the expectation. I was in sales, and had to act bubbly, talkative, and articulate, for the client's sake. Don't get me wrong, I had really good relationships with girlfriends, but was still not very open. I didn't allow myself to be fully known, which was tied to the abortion and molestation. I didn't tell anyone about Douglas the lifeguard until decades later. Though I'd told my mom what my stepfather had done to me, I continued to carry my secret about him.

There is a similar trait with people who have been

molested. Some carry a chip on their shoulder, they are not always nice or kind. A protective shield and hardened shell are common. Erecting a wall makes one less approachable, and that tough exterior keeps others from seeing the inner ruins.

My dear friend Valerie, used to say, "Well you know you are like the ice princess, Tegra." She called it right on out, and I would look at her and roll my eyes. I didn't like it at all because her statement did not feel like a compliment. I defined being an ice princess as being cold and standoffish. One can be flawlessly dressed and look beautiful on the outside, but the Ice Princess wearing an irregular tag sits at the perimeter, waiting for a breach. I was a damaged Ice Princess. Don't let anyone get too close, that was my protection.

Being cold drove away the deeper relationships I could have had. There were one or two women that came into my circle who were deeply wounded and going through it. I just didn't have it in me to give them what they needed. I had limited supply of empathy and compassion. A spirit of abortion influenced me to discount relationships and throw them aside. I acted with compassion when it was the right thing to do. I operated this way knowing I had my little discipleship circle of friends. If they were not in the discipleship group, I didn't have extra time or energy to extend myself further. If I went deeper with their stuff, I would have to go deeper with my own. I did not want to do that because I might be judged by them. Pure narcissism.

Robert Brown and my husband Marc have been lifelong friends. Marc and I had only been dating for six or seven months when he became involved with a fashion show production at USC's Bouvard Auditorium. He is a wonderful singer and was singing a song during a show one evening. Somehow, he tripped and fell off the stage. After gathering himself, he exited to the backstage area where Robert and some of his friends were waiting for him. It was my first time meeting some of them, and I offered the coldest handshake I could muster. If that cold, limp handshake could have spoken it would have said, "I don't want to be here, and I certainly don't want to talk to you or shake your hand. I just want to get out of here." The next morning Marc said, "You know the way you shook the hands of my two friends last night? Well, Robert noticed you gave them limp handshakes and were standoffish. Are you okay?" I told him I was fine. He didn't try to unpack it with me, but it did give him pause. He had not seen me act this way in our short time of dating. My Ice Princess character flaw needed to be addressed, but I guess he decided to laugh it off and leave it alone.

Now I recognize it right away in others. I am thankful for the deeper growth in Christ, discipleship, and accountability to other women in the circle. I was able to blossom and become who Christ created me to be. I can readily discern that destructive spirit because I was roommates with it. It's good to be delivered from shame, to be fully known and present. I have been walking this way for almost twenty years now and it's liberating and refreshing.

I recently had a conversation with my husband Marc about the whole "ice princess" moniker Valerie placed on me. He said he didn't really see it as a negative and didn't believe Valerie did either. He felt she was coming from more of a "diva" perspective. I reminded him I never accepted labels like that and that when I met his friends after his performance that night, he voiced that he thought I was pretty cold. He said, "Babe, yes you were pretty cold that night, but that is the night you tried to break up with me." The memory came flooding back. He went on to remind me about my bad attitude. You see, I had this cute little raggedy Volkswagen Bug and he had a '67 Mustang, and something was wrong with both of our cars. He reminded me that I wanted to kick him to the curb because he was a broke young college student. We had gone to an on-campus party after his performance that night. As we stood on the balcony, I told him we weren't going to work anymore because he was broke, and I made sure to toss in some other mean things as well. All kinds of light bulbs were beginning to go off in my mind about that night. I never dated guys my age. The guys I dated were older and more established, probably because I was looking for a father figure. As I continued my diatribe, he started laughing in my face and not taking me seriously. I couldn't believe he was laughing while I was trying to be serious about cutting off the relationship. When he brought this to my remembrance I said, "Oh yeah, I do remember always having such a bad attitude about any and everything." I asked him if he felt I exuded the type of behavior Valerie was talking about? He said yes, there were times even after our marriage when I could be very standoffish with people. He felt I should use a different adjective to describe the behavior. He suggested "circumspect." Pondering on it a bit, I believe that is very true. He still sees me as very circumspect when feeling people out. I don't allow people to get too close until I feel right about them in my spirit. I was glad I spoke with him about it, as he gave me insight into some things I hadn't considered. I evolved to become circumspect as opposed to deprecating.

Chapter Six

Trapped by Shame

SHAME IS SATAN'S PLAYGROUND, LASER-HONED ON God's greatest creation with the intent to kill, steal, and destroy purpose. It is like a missile aimed to strike at God's very heart, the human race. So many things are aborted in the five-to-ten-minute procedure. Dreams are disrupted, visions are distorted, and relationships become strained. Women and men tend to think they can move on with life after it's done and everything will be totally fine, not understanding the inevitable fallout.

> *Shame is probably the most difficult and debilitating emotion that there is. Shame tells us that we are not okay and that there is something deeply wrong with us that cannot be fixed or cured. When we feel shame, it is as if there is a stain on us that we cannot remove. Shame separates us from other people for it requires secrecy to survive.*
>
> (LEHR, 2018, PAR. 11)

There are so many women who have abortions, gone through our ministry, and received healing. Some women that have children after they have had an abortion have strained relationships with the children that they birthed later in life. I have heard many stories regarding the division that takes place. It gets better but must be worked on. They think, *"I'm not worthy to be a mother because I killed the child/children before I had this child."* They may feel a lack of natural closeness and push them away, or some mothers may smother their children. I myself experienced feelings of unworthiness with my own son, Yakob. When Marc and I went to Ethiopia to receive him, I became ill. I had a very bad case of the flu the last two or three days before we were scheduled to return to the U.S. Prior to this trip, we had lost a baby girl from an Ethiopian orphanage. This added to my anxiety, as the mourning process was intense. A day or two before we were to board the plane to return to the U.S. with Yakob as a family, a fear came over me and I began to feel like something tragic was going to happen. The loss of Rahel, and maybe even my own past abortion, took their toll. I don't know. I didn't smother him, but I didn't want him out of my sight either. I was a little manic and just wanted to get back onto American soil. Getting back to my home, where I could feel comfortable and safe, was my goal.

My mom was waiting at the house for us when we got home. As soon as I walked through the front door and down the stairs, I sat down on the couch and all I could do was break down and cry. I was so glad to be home and safe. I used to physically shake sometimes when talking about it and didn't know what was happening. I believe I was dealing with the residue of shame, that marker of sin I had created, and had to be very introspective. I needed to immediately cleanse whatever was trying to overtake me emotionally during that moment.

The shame of abortion, whether brought on by our own actions or assigned to us by demonic influence, endeavors to abort everything you want to accomplish in life. It affects everything and can be blinding. The enemy of our souls wants us isolated and away from our community to more easily infiltrate our minds with deceptive thoughts and lies. He then has room to slither about without the interference of good influence from others. We must have community in our lives.

God put great thought into us as our Creator. We are His masterpieces, fearfully and wonderfully made. Our stories were divinely crafted before the foundations of the world were laid and the devil hates it. He can't stand anything made in the image of God, the *Imago Dei*, so his motive is to kill it. He is angry and seeks revenge by working to keep us in bondage in our minds. One of the things Minister Traci used to say that made so much sense to me was, "I am sorry, but the enemy cannot pack his bag and come park himself in my thoughts. He has paid no rent nor mortgage. He has paid nothing, so he has to leave." She is correct! The enemy is a squatter on property that does not belong to him. The only thing he has is what God allows and uses for his greater purpose.

I received a call one morning from Bethany, a woman traumatized by past events. She was dating and deeply in love with an unmarried associate pastor at her church for a few years. She was certain they were going to get married. When her pregnancy test came back positive and she shared the news with her beau, she never thought he would twist her arm into aborting the child. Bethany could not understand why he wanted her to abort their baby. He was unwilling to marry her at that time even though he tricked her into believing his love was genuine. He drove her to the clinic, in the car she owned, and dropped her off for the procedure. He did not walk in with her. Instead, he told her he would return at the appropriate time to pick her up and drive her home. After the procedure, Bethany patiently waited in the waiting room for at least two hours. She phoned him several times, but he never answered. The clinic was closing so she walked outside to wait a bit longer only to realize he was not going to show up. Bethany finally called a cab. When she arrived home her car was in the driveway and the car keys were placed in her mailbox. This was the last time she ever saw or heard from him. He completely disappeared.

> *Guilt says: I made a mistake. Shame says: I am a mistake.*
>
> MAX LUCADO

As I listened to Bethany's story, I thought of the story of Tamar in 2 SAMUEL 13:19. Tamar was raped by her brother, Amnon, and then discarded like a piece of trash. She walked away devastated, cloaked in shame. Bethany was not raped, but she was abandoned by someone she thought loved her. Her shame ushered her into a decade of isolation. She devalued herself and was afraid of judgment and condemnation from others. Bethany thought there was safety in her community of one, which was herself.

Bethany's story is not uncommon. The enemy of our souls does his best work when we choose to isolate ourselves from others. He's quick to slap on labels such as "unworthy", "unlovable", "unforgiveable", "unredeemable", "defeated", "hopeless", "a failure", and "forgotten." The uninvited guests of shame and fear move into our thoughts and create a fortress of secrecy. Shame is allowed to grow when we don't talk about it; those who are most shame-laden assume their experience of shame is unique and isolating.

The Stronghold of Secrecy

Shame begets secrecy and secrecy begets isolation. Where there is secrecy, there can be no accountability over our behavior. Many participants in our group drank alcohol to numb their pain and they did so in secrecy. Some also medicated themselves with pills and promiscuity. They had lost their motivation. Some weren't organized in their thoughts and their living spaces. The secrecy surrounding abortion is a stronghold because the enemy wants to keep us silent from talking about this issue. Secrecy is rooted in pride because we fear judgement, especially from family. But many women learn their children and/or siblings have had abortions, and the code of silence breaks, and the captives are set free in that family. We encourage our groups to share their stories with family members to help break the cycle within their bloodline. Some of their parents have also confessed to having had abortions. It becomes a spiraling domino effect, an epidemic. I believe it is so critically important for people who have had abortions to share it with whomever God leads them to share it with. Particularly our families with young adults. By not sharing, the risk of them running to the abortion clinic to repeat the cycle increases. The stronghold of secrecy must be broken as a part of the pathway to healing.

When God called me to start No Longer Bound, I chose to share my testimony with two of my teenaged nieces. At the time they were young women who were intellectually and spiritually old enough to comprehend my message. I wanted them to know that sanctity of life was important to me. We don't always make wise decisions and if anyone in my family was tempted to even contemplate abortion, they knew from me it certainly was not an option. When Yakob was two years old, I showed him a tiny model of a fetus in its earliest developmental stage. I asked him, "Honey, what is this?" In the sweetest tone he answered, "A baby!" At two years old, it was clear to him what a baby looks like. We constantly talk to him about the importance of life and the dynamics of a mother carrying a baby in her tummy. He knows what No Longer Bound is all about, how we help people get better and can articulate our mission in his own way. It is critically important to share these stories with whomever God leads, particularly the young adults in our families. We must sear into their minds that abortion is not an option!

The stronghold of secrecy resembles depression, low self-esteem, self-loathing, and no motivation. It's wretchedly hypnotic and paralyzing. Wallowing in secrecy is difficult to shake and can drive one into isolation. We're only as sick as our secrets, but we can successfully gain a breakthrough in this area. Confession is good for the soul.

> *Confess your sins to each other and pray for each other so that you may be healed. The earnest prayer of a righteous person has great power and produces wonderful results.*
>
> James 5:16, NLT

Finding someone or a group who can be trusted is the first step. Being part of a group to share with others wounded by the pain of abortion is beneficial. Their stories have the potential to trigger another's inward struggle and loosen psychological debris. Even introverts, when they are pushed, say it's the best thing they've ever done. They blossom within the group setting. The group does something new for them. Acceptance and empathy permeate throughout the atmosphere within a safe place.

> *Without good direction, people lose their way; the more wise counsel you follow, the better your chances.*
>
> PROVERBS 11:14, MSG

The Stronghold of Division

Relationships struggle behind the diabolical intent strewn by the stronghold of division. In marriages, one partner may reveal abortion was in their background. Sometimes the wife doesn't know her husband had abortion in his background because it happened with someone else prior to their marriage. Once the secret is uncovered, a strained relationship can begin the process of healing. For parents, the need for healing is uncovered after their sons or daughters have first gone through their healing process. The stronghold of division has a root hidden in secrecy. Its devices leak into various levels and hierarchies of the family.

I know a woman who thought her relationship with her mother was close, yet felt it needed to be deepened. She finally shared her healing story with her mother, who in turn revealed she also had abortion in her background. The mother began to attend bible study with her daughter and soon decided to attend a healing retreat. Since going on the retreat, the mother/daughter relationship has grown to be stronger and deeper than ever! Their hearts are knit together in new ways. The hurt and pain needed to be dealt with and eradicated. Now the mother tells her story to every family member she can, and anyone else she is led to share her story with. The mother is free and desires the same for others!

Silence can become an ally with the enemy. The stronghold of division is multi-layered and once removed, room for pure love and a deeper level of intimacy is beautifully discovered.

As matters begin to unfold and come into perspective, I pose questions to the women and men who sign up for No Longer Bound: "Tell me your story before the abortion. Did you dream? Did you have friends and community? Were you sociable and did you have a very positive outlook for your future?" Almost all say yes. Then I ask what happened after the abortion. They say they ended up alone, and their dreams and visions became a thing of the past. But after they received their healing, all said they had clarity. They could hear God's voice. Their mantras became, "I can do it!" So many ladies went back to school to get their master's degrees because they felt like conquerors. After the abortions, their belief in themselves is so very low, but when healing takes place, they believe they are *more* than conquerors!

My Arsenal

God always offers us an alternative to the way we live our lives. There's nothing more powerful than my arsenal, which is the word of God, to combat shame. Whenever shame appears, I know it's rendered powerless in the presence of Christ. Every time I had a setback in my journey to motherhood, the enemy would slither in to condemn me and whisper lies regarding my abortion as the reason for my delayed blessing. Clearly moments of spiritual warfare. My best defense was to replace those lies with God's truth. I had to continue to believe I would bear fruit throughout my life:

The Vine and the Branches

I am the true vine, and my Father is the gardener. He cuts off every branch in me that bears no fruit, while every branch that does bear fruit, he prunes so that it will be even more fruitful. You are already clean because of the word I have spoken to you. Remain in me, as I also remain in you. No branch can bear fruit by itself; it must remain in the vine. Neither can you bear fruit unless you remain in me.

I am the vine; you are the branches. If you remain in me and I in you, you will bear much fruit; apart from me you can do nothing. If you do not remain in me, you are like a branch that is thrown away and withers; such branches are picked up, thrown into the fire and burned. If you remain in me and my words remain in you, ask whatever you wish, and it will be done for you. This is to my Father's glory, that you bear much fruit, showing yourselves to be my disciples.

JOHN 15:1-8, NIV

I had to renew my mind to make certain my thoughts were laser focused and not thrown off course:

Finally, brothers and sisters, whatever is true, whatever is noble, whatever is right, whatever is pure, whatever is lovely, whatever is admirable—if anything is excellent or praiseworthy—think about such things.

PHILIPPIANS 4:8, NIV

I had to believe everything God was showing me:

> *Call to Me, and I will answer you, and show you great and mighty things, which you do not know.*
>
> JEREMIAH 33:3, NKJV

I had to believe God was ordering and directing my paths:

> *Trust in the Lord with all your heart, and lean not on your own understanding; in all your ways acknowledge Him, and He shall direct your paths.*
>
> PROVERBS 3:5-6, NKJV

I had to believe what God promised me:

> *Blessed is she who has believed that the Lord would fulfill his promises to her!*
>
> LUKE 1:45, NIV

His Grace

"A Woman Caught in Adultery" is a powerful depiction of Jesus' divine mercy, redemption, acceptance, and love for us. The woman caught in adultery was not judged, discarded, hated or shamed by Jesus. I am thankful for the same grace offered to her was and still is extended to me and you daily for our sin of abortion.

A Woman Caught in Adultery

> *Jesus returned to the Mount of Olives, but early the next morning he was back again at the Temple. A crowd soon gathered, and he sat down and taught them. As he was speaking, the teachers of religious law and the Pharisees*

> *brought a woman who had been caught in the act of adultery. They put her in front of the crowd.*
>
> *"Teacher," they said to Jesus, "this woman was caught in the act of adultery. The law of Moses says to stone her. What do you say?"*
>
> *They were trying to trap him into saying something they could use against him, but Jesus stooped down and wrote in the dust with his finger. They kept demanding an answer, so he stood up again and said, "All right, but let the one who has never sinned throw the first stone!" Then he stooped down again and wrote in the dust.*
>
> *When the accusers heard this, they slipped away one by one, beginning with the oldest, until only Jesus was left in the middle of the crowd with the woman. Then Jesus stood up again and said to the woman, "Where are your accusers? Didn't even one of them condemn you?" "No, Lord," she said. And Jesus said, "Neither do I. Go and sin no more."*
>
> JOHN 8:1-11, NLT

Unmasking shame is a very effective way to strip away its power. God's grace and forgiveness covers a multitude of sin. He wants us to leave our shameful past and trust Him for the future. Jesus died on the cross for our sin and he's the only one able to cleanse away our shame.

Chapter Seven

Silent Sorrow

In December of 2004, I had another molar pregnancy. Of course, at first, I was just excited I was pregnant, as I wasn't aware of my predicament. The fall and winter seasons always seemed to be the time I had to deal with pregnancy issues. When I got the call from my doctor in late December, he told me there was no fetus and that he would need to do a D&C. I said "Okay, no problem." I had the procedure and felt like, been there, done that, here we go again. My doctor told me I would need to take methotrexate chemotherapy shots after surgery to get rid of the human chorionic gonadotropin hormone (HCG), also called the pregnancy hormone, something I didn't have to do with my first molar pregnancy because there had been no issues. But this time my hormone count was at 20,000 when it should have been at zero. The problem was I still had pregnancy tissue lodged in the lining of my uterine wall. I asked my doctor about the side effects. He knew me to be a health nut and said I would be fine and shouldn't experience any, maybe just a little sluggish here and there. I gave the green light. He thought I would only need to get the methotrexate shot every week for thirty to sixty days. I was fine with his explanation and felt I could handle what was ahead. That was in January.

June rolled around and I was still taking the shot. This was definitely a significant problem. My hormone count had dropped to under 5000 but wasn't moving closer to zero as it should have in that time frame. I chose not to panic, but believed I needed to be more assertive in taking matters into my own hands. Again, I received a call from my doctor saying, "You know what Tegra, it looks like your count is taking a turn for the worse and we are probably going to have to do aggressive chemotherapy and probably a hysterectomy." I thought, "You cannot be serious? I am not adhering to any of that." He probably thought I was crazy, but so what! I said, "No, this is what I am going to do. I am going to do some research on an all-raw detox center in San Diego. I think it is best for me to go spend time there, get cleansed on a cellular level, and then we will see where I am." He told me that I didn't want to play around with this because I didn't want anything to spread to my lungs or my brain. I knew I needed to check myself into the detox center.

I really did feel the Lord was leading me there and everything was going to be okay, so I told Marc. He told me plain and simple he was not about to lose me to some holistic unscientific theory. What was happening with me was serious and I needed to get the chemo then we'd see where we were. I told him he needed to hear what I was saying and what I heard from the Lord as well. His prescription for me was not what I was supposed to take. I called Minister Traci and a few more of my prayer warrior sisters to gather and pray on the day I received the information. Minister Traci asked me what I wanted to do. I answered, "Well I want to go to the detox center. I believe everything will be fine, but Marc is not on the same page with me." Minister Traci talked with Marc and he said, "Okay how long is the program?" I said, "The full program is three weeks at least." My doctor said if I chose to take that route, he wanted me to check in with a local hospital to have my blood work done weekly so he could monitor everything. Marc calmed down and said, "Okay fine, three weeks, and don't ask for anything longer."

I checked myself into the Optimum Health Institute for my detox, and what a completely different experience it was. Such a beautiful facility with a slight "new age" leaning, but I didn't care. I was walking in with the Holy Spirit so I knew all would be fine. My first week there I had my blood work done at the local hospital and my count dropped to 1000. This was a miracle in my eyes and confirmed my reason for coming to Optimum Health. This was the right thing for me to do. Marc was in awe as well. My doctor said we would continue to keep an eye on things but didn't want to get too excited. The second week my count increased to 10,000 but I still didn't care because I was feeling good and believed all things were working together for my good. I was fine, had a room to myself, played my worship music, and prayed in the presence of the Lord. More than ever, I felt I was supposed to be there and tethered to the Lord by myself. Week three came and my count was 30,000, yet I still did not care. Marc was ready for me to come home but I held on to what I believed the Holy Spirit was directing me to do.

I met a sweet, beautiful Christian woman from Denver,

CO who was also doing the program and we befriended one another. I told her I did not have children but held a deep desire to become a mother. She was there because she just wanted to clean her system and have more children. I explained I was there because I wanted to have children and needed to cleanse my system to hopefully avoid having a hysterectomy. Then seemingly out of left field she said, "I had an abortion." I stopped in my tracks. Astonished I said, "What did you say?" She repeated, "Oh girl, I had an abortion." Well, I'd never heard anyone say that other than my friend Nathan. I'm sure I had that "deer in headlights" look on my face. She continued, "Yes Tegra, but you know what? When Jesus was nailed to that cross, my abortion was nailed to the cross too." I felt emboldened to tell her my secret, "Oh my gosh, I had an abortion too and now I am having a lot of fertility problems." She said, "Girl, your abortion was nailed to the cross as well, Tegra." That gripped me to my core. When I look back it is clear I needed that down in my soul. We left one another in the courtyard, I went back to my room and she back to hers.

Once I got back to my room, I sobbed so hard. I wanted and needed to talk to Marc. I was in a desperate space where I needed to commune with my husband. He was traveling to Cuba and I could not reach him, so I called another dear friend who is an evangelist and a mighty woman of God. I told her what was going on but didn't share anything about the abortion. I just told her I needed Marc and she said, "Honey, I understand how you are feeling. You are longing for your covering right now." I told her I didn't know what was going to happen to me and my count was not going down. My doctor said I was going to need a full hysterectomy and maybe chemotherapy. She calmed me down and prayed fervently for me over the phone and we talked for an hour. Immediately after we hung up, Marc called. I shared with him how much I needed to talk with him and that I did not know what was going to happen to me. One thing that was obviously clear, it was time for me to come back home and have another meeting with Dr. Lee, my oncologist out of Cedars-Sinai. Marc would be returning from Cuba in the next four days.

Shortly after returning home, I told my doctor I needed to meet with a top molar pregnancy specialist. In doing so, I would be able to make the best decision. I loved talking to my doctor, but I needed an extra opinion. He referred me to Cedars-Sinai's top molar pregnancy specialist, Dr. Leuchter. I met with the specialist and he said, "Tegra, I've looked at everything. Your hydration levels look great, your red blood cell count, white blood cell count, everything looks good, but you cannot avoid the surgery. Based on my experience, if you avoid the surgery this could spread, but because your blood work looks great, hydration and cell levels all look great, you are not going to need to have a full hysterectomy. I'm recommending a partial hysterectomy so that you can keep your ovaries and you and your husband can still have children." I asked him about the chemotherapy because I didn't want to hear anything about a gestational surrogate at that point. He told me I would probably only need two to three days of chemo and that should be it. The next day my HCG count was at 183,000 and climbing. The peace that passes all understanding was guarding my heart and assured me everything was going to be just fine. A week and a half later Marc returned from his trip and I was ready for the surgery.

After surgery, I was wheeled into my room at the hospital and had tons of energy. I was walking the corridors praying for people in their rooms. I was surprised at myself as this was quite different for me. Marc would watch me, probably thinking, "*What is my wife doing?*" I would go from room to room, stretch my hand out over the people as they lay in their beds and just pray. It wasn't meant for me to lie in bed because I wasn't down and out. I needed to get up and move. The Lord blessed me to do ministry for the three or four days I was there.

When I came back home Dr. Lee said, "I'm going to need you to come back every couple of days to check your HCG count so we can make sure the number is going down." I said okay, and two to three weeks later it hit zero which was such a praise report. I was thrilled. Dr. Lee said I would have to wait for the pathology report to come back and when it returned everything looked fine. Still, it was recommended by the pathologist that I receive radiation just to make sure. I said, "Dr. Lee, you know I am not doing that." On my behalf he told them I would not undergo radiation but asked me to come back every three to four months to check my blood work and make sure everything was okay. He assured me I would be fine, and I believed him.

In October 2004, I was determined completely cancer-free. It was also in October 2004 that the Holy Spirit told me I would be entering into a season of loneliness. I didn't understand what he meant at the time, but it soon became clear.

The Gestational Surrogacy Journey

At our last attempt with gestational surrogacy Bishop Ulmer called me when I was on my way to the clinic and said, "Tegra you have to ask yourself, do you want to have a baby, or do you just want to be a mother however God wants to bless you to do so?" He was basically saying, if surrogacy doesn't work, I was going to need to sit with the outcome and ask myself that real question. I heard him but at the same time, I was on my way to the hospital to get my eggs transferred. I understood Bishop Ulmer planted a seed that would ultimately germinate.

We probably started gestational surrogacy in 2007 and it was not an easy process. Even though we were using my eggs and Marc's sperm, someone else would be carrying the baby for us. There were friends in my circle who were a bit younger than me who said, "You know what, Tegra? Maybe I should carry the baby for you." Marc and I felt it was best to go through the normal channels. It would have been too close for comfort with a friend. We signed up at a highly regarded surrogacy agency and I had a great endocrinologist. So many people use him, he's like a rock star and has the look to boot!

The surrogacy agency we used matched us with two or three couples to interview. We liked that they also had children of their own. They were Christians who felt called to surrogacy and were all very sweet. The one girl we chose made the embryo transfer. We waited and waited and waited, wondering if she would ever get pregnant. Unfortunately, it didn't take. She did not get pregnant. Another blow. This procedure is quite costly, so we needed to step back and reevaluate our process. We decided to try again and with the next attempt, my eggs didn't take. The sperm and egg need to come together in the petri dish, but it did not work and was considered a failed cycle.

By this time, we had another gestational surrogate because the first one had decided to move on. When you connect with someone and don't move forward in two or three months, that surrogate has the choice to move on to a different family and we were fine with her decision. We weren't ready to jump back into another cycle so quickly because it was exhausting and devastating. We needed time to just wait and not rush into the next process. When the petri dish attempt didn't work for the second surrogate, I was heartbroken once again. That was it! We were now at the point where it was just too pricey and not working out for all of us. What was going on? This was going to be our third and final attempt with our second gestational surrogate who was absolutely amazing. I was going through acupuncture treatment with a therapist and drove out to Westlake every week for almost three months. I felt desperate this particular time. I had four really great embryos from what the doctor said, and he inserted all four into this gestational surrogate. Four embryos are quite frankly a lot. Before we decided to do this last treatment, I was probably forty-three years old, so the doctor's recommendation was for me to use donor eggs. Marc and I didn't believe donor eggs were for us and I was glad we were on the same page. Other friends of ours selected this route, but after prayerful consideration, the option wasn't for us. We both felt good about the four embryos being inserted into our surrogate and she felt good about it as well. We were all praying, and it seemed like it was going to work. Three weeks later she called and said it didn't take. By now we were both sitting looking at each other. We had come to the end of our road and knew we couldn't afford to go any further.

We knew we were not going with donor eggs and needed to press the pause button to figure out our next move. After all of this the enemy started to creep back into my psyche. *"Yeah, this is punishment because of your abortion."* Instead of me changing the tape in my mind to *"There are consequences to the bad choices we make,"* I allowed my opponent's voice to linger in an incessant rehearsal of doom. *"Yeah, because you had the abortion that's why you're having problems, that's why you can't be a mother, that's why you can't have a baby, because you murdered your baby."* How much more of this can a person take? Our last attempt was in 2009. We pressed the pause button and talked about adoption but didn't *really* talk about it. It was on the table but not unpacked.

Ethiopia

In 2012, I decided to take a trip to Ethiopia by myself with Youth With A Mission, a very well-known mission organization. I had started doing some research and I found them while tinkering online. This organization had an adoption arm out of Ethiopia. This was remarkable! They had mission trips to Ethiopia with one coming up in three months. My thoughts were swirling, *"I know I'm supposed to go on this mission trip because I've always had a passion for Ethiopia."* It all started when I was twenty years old, but I didn't understand it at the time. I was drawn to the culture and the kids because I used to see a variety of stories on TV back in the day. I used to wonder when I'd visit the country and what I would do there. Was I supposed to adopt? Was I supposed to go on a mission trip? I didn't think about it again until I found YWAM.

I called and began communicating with staff and found them to be wonderful. The woman I spoke with said they had a mission trip coming up in June and I asked if they still had space. She said yes, there were only two or three spaces left and if I wanted to go with them, I needed to turn in my paperwork as soon as possible. This was big for me because I hadn't traveled internationally by myself with people I didn't know. It's one thing traveling domestically and quite another internationally. She asked me about my background and was I doing anything in ministry. I told her about No Longer Bound and she said, "Oh my gosh Tegra, the first crisis pregnancy center and home for pregnant girls is in Ethiopia." I replied, "What are you talking about?" She answered, "It's in Ethiopia and we are affiliated with it." I said, "You have got to be kidding me!" She said, "I think this is a God thing for you." "Ya think?" I playfully responded. She is incredible. I told her I was in and then told Marc about the conversation. He said, "Babe you've got to go."

I found out there were women and men coming in from the UK that were going to be part of our team. There were some coming in from the state of Washington and I was the only one traveling from California. At the end of the day, I think there were probably about fifteen to twenty of us. The trip was absolutely amazing! I felt for the first time, out of all my travels to the various African countries I have visited, that Ethiopia was home. There was a kinship unlike any other I've ever experienced on the continent of Africa. I felt it from the time I got off the plane and people were talking to me in Amharic. I would say, "No, no, no, I'm a black American." They said, "No, you are actually Ethiopian." There was such a love, affection and affinity there that I just fell in love with the people, the food, and the country. Then of course I fell in love with a church there. The pastor, the evangelists, all of it. The pinnacle for me though was falling in love with the home for unwed pregnant girls. Genet, my Ethiopian sister, was heading up the organization there and as soon as I met her, I fell in love with her too! The girls at the center were very young. Some of them were sixteen, seventeen, or eighteen years old. I found out some of the girls that get pregnant may have their baby in the bush somewhere and then leave the child for the hyenas to attack. They do this because of the shame in getting pregnant and having to tell their family. In order to avoid the shame, they usually wear large clothing and have the baby sequestered away.

It was beautiful just being there and hanging out at the home. All of the girls were friendly. I was able to lay hands on them, pray, and affirm their decision to keep their children. They also made handmade jewelry to sell so they could have money to do whatever they wanted with it, which was really nice. I kept wanting to go back to the home for unwed girls every day. That was my hang spot! I spent seven days there and it was the most wonderful trip. Marc just had to come back with me the next time. I told Julia from YWAM that I wanted to bring a group of friends with me when I returned with Marc, but she preferred for Marc and me to come together first. Just the two of us with her and another YWAM leader, Ahmed, who could take us wherever we needed to go. She called it a vision trip where we would pray and ask the Lord to reveal how He would use us, then put a plan together for the group. That resonated with me.

In April 2013, Marc and I traveled to Ethiopia together. Ahmed was there and took us to visit different Muslim villages where this organization ministers to those who have converted from Islam to Christianity. It was beautiful to meet the men, women, and families in those villages. We ministered and encouraged them and once again saw the beautiful children. Julia opened a new orphanage in this particular area of Ethiopia, and we got to meet even more children!

During my first trip we visited several different orphanages as well. Ahmed really wanted us to meet with Genet so on our second-to-last day there he escorted us to see her. As he was driving, he said, "Well, there is a baby there." I asked, "What do you mean?" He replied, "Genet knows you and Marc are here, and there is a young seventeen-year-old girl who had a baby literally six days ago. Because she is so young, her family wants her to give the baby up for adoption. We think it's perfect that you both are here, because we want you to meet the mother and adopt baby Rahel!" We arrived to find Genet's face lit with a smile from ear-to-ear. She exclaimed, "Yes, this is a God thing, it's obvious! I mean, how else could this come into play." We were excited and instantly decided, okay, let's go!

Mother and daughter were there when we arrived. The mother, named Nyala, was a beautiful young teenaged girl who didn't speak a lick of English. She only spoke Amharic, so thank goodness there were others there who helped interpret. Genet continued spouting that this was a divine set-up, that God was in the mix of it all, and we agreed. The little girl was simply precious, and it felt right. We spent hours there with Genet, Nyala, and Rahel. All of us together were a little family. Nyala had tried to abort the child by taking some sort of Coca-Cola concoction her crazy friends told her to take, and it failed. Then she decided to go to the abortion clinic. Thank goodness Genet had a relationship with this particular clinic. A couple of the ladies who worked there would call her sometimes and say, "There's a young woman here, you may want to come and intervene." This doesn't happen in the U.S.! This is why Rahel was saved. We all felt we were standing right in the middle of a miracle!

On our last day in Ethiopia, Marc was holding our soon-to-be adopted daughter. We noticed she was looking directly at his face and into his eyes with a piercing gaze. There was a message in her stare, a love connection that immediately tucked itself into our hearts. We hit the ground running as soon as we returned from Ethiopia. We gathered all of the adoption paperwork, dotted all the i's and crossed every t in one week flat, which is not the norm. Our stuff was moving! We were in the queue to start getting approvals and told Julia and Ahmed we wanted to send formula specifically for Rahel. Julia agreed and we donated money online that was forwarded to Ahmed for him to purchase her formula. All was right with the world.

We were told her formula was being sent to another orphanage because Rahel was being transferred. I'm still not clear why she was transferred. We met the man who was head of that orphanage and trusted everything would be fine. Two weeks later, we got a call informing us that Rahel was sick. Ahmed told us he was going to check on her and made us feel she would probably be just fine but offered to personally check on her. He found her doing well. One week later, she was back in the hospital and this time it was extremely serious. Rahel had sepsis and her body was shutting down. Unbelievable! Two of our Ethiopian friends that live in the U.S. got involved to help us communicate with the hospital. The wife of one of our friends is a nurse and said this was truly a bad situation. I was perplexed and didn't understand how something like this could have happened. Rahel was dehydrated and not getting the vitamins and minerals she needed, but how could this be? We were paying to send formula to the orphanage. Ahmed emailed us the next day and told us the orphanage director went out of town and Rahel's formula was locked in a closet. They were watering down formula in the orphanage in order to feed all of the babies. Well, no wonder she was dehydrated and not getting the vitamins and minerals she needed! Our beautiful baby girl died the next day. She was only nine weeks old.

I just couldn't believe this was happening and began reliving the trauma. It was severely painful and although I am healed, it still hurts when I think about it. I was in a state of grief unlike never before. We received a call from Marc's mom, who said, "I don't know what to say." She called us back that night and said, "I don't know if I'm supposed to say this, but the Lord told me that Rahel was not for you and Marc. You were there for her so she could feel the love of parents before she went into eternity." Her words brought us a level of comfort we had not experienced during this process. She truly ministered to us, but I was still in a dark place. Marc took time off work but eventually had to go back. I was at the house by myself in a state of deep depression. I could not even open my bible or pray. I was literally handicapped, but the Lord sent my community to pray, worship, and speak words of encouragement into my life. That is what kept me from sinking and what fed my empty soul.

A month later I talked with a father of one of our leadership team members from No Longer Bound. He had also gone through the program in 2012. He called me and pretty much repeated the same words Marc's mother had shared with us. We hadn't told anyone what she said. He received that word from the Holy Spirit as well. This was a confirmation. He told us the Lord told him to share it. What a blessing that was.

I had harbored a deep hatred towards the orphanage

director. How could he have locked up her formula and not leave the key? It was beyond my comprehension. Then once again that wicked refrain crept through my mind, *"You are being punished because of your abortion. That is why she died."* I had already gotten my healing and was deep into the ministry, but the enemy was trying to get my eyes off of God and focus on the dark words he was trying to deposit into my spirit. I allowed that deposit to come in for a little while. I fellowshipped with it. But when I am weak, my God shows himself strong. Ultimately, I became stronger and stronger.

In September 2013, the Lord told me I was going to return to Ethiopia in December to visit the orphanage director and apologize to him for the feelings I had toward him. He told me I would ask for forgiveness, and I would forgive him too. I told the Lord, *"No, I'm not doing that. I can't do that!"* But I had enough sense to know the Lord had already spoken, and it was not a favor he was asking of me. It was a command and if I didn't follow through with it, I would be walking in disobedience. I told Marc what happened, and he said, "I don't care Tegra, I am not going to Ethiopia to sit in front of Geremew because I really don't know what I will do to him." I said, "So you want me to go to Ethiopia by myself? Because I have to go" He said, "Yeah, you will go, and I won't." I couldn't believe he was going to let me do this by myself, but in the back of my mind I felt he would change his mind. But it did not matter if he didn't go because that's what the Lord said to me. He did not say that Marc had to accompany me.

I started going back to therapy sessions because I needed help. I was still in a dark place and therapy was helping me get stronger. November began to roll around and Marc said we would go back to Ethiopia together. I was surprised but thankful he had changed his mind. I'm sure the Lord spoke to his heart.

We arrived back in Ethiopia in December to meet with Geremew, the orphanage director, along with the interpreter/driver whom we befriended during our prior trip. Upon our arrival at the orphanage, Geremew was waiting for us outside with the traditional snack of popcorn, sparkling cider, and coffee. At first, we just sat and stared at each other for a little while. I started talking to open things up. I apologized and told him what the Lord told me I had to do. I said, "I am sorry that I harbored anger and hatred and resentment and bitterness toward you. I am terribly sorry." I cried, and by this time Geremew and Marc were crying too. Through the interpreter, Geremew kept apologizing. He didn't understand what had happened and was deeply wounded and apologetic. I can't even imagine how he must have felt because basically it was due to his negligence that Rahel died. The weight he must have been carrying could not be explained. He needed me to verbally share that with him. He needed to be free, and for us to be able to go and make amends was real time ministry happening before our very eyes. He became my brother that I had to love and there was a genuine kinship. We were like family sitting at that table. When we got up to leave, we were hugging, laughing, and smiling. All of the bitterness, anger, hatred, and resentment was gone. The Lord got the glory.

Geremew told us there were children at his orphanage in need of adoption and suggested we look at some of the kids right there. Marc and I didn't feel it was the appropriate time, because that was not what we came for. Geremew continued to insist we come inside, and we finally acquiesced. Of course, we saw the most beautiful children. He asked us to come back the next day because there was a mother of a baby that he wanted us to meet. We still didn't feel right about it, but we came back anyway. We met the mother, but it still wasn't right. We did get to meet with Nyala again and this time with more of her family members who we didn't have the opportunity to meet the first time. We were able to meet the aunt and uncle who had basically raised her and shared with them all that had happened. They were very sad and together we all cried more tears. We let them know we paid for Rahel's headstone and had pictures of it but wanted to go to the actual grave site with them as none of them had gone yet. Ahmed and Genet worked it out so we could all go and grieve together. As sad as it may seem, ours was a beautiful gathering of hearts and something we will forever hold dear.

Marc and I returned home in December 2013. In June 2014 we got a referral from the agency for Yakob but there was a snafu. We received the referral from the agency before we got pictures of him. They were delighted and said, "Oh my, Tegra, you are going to love Yakob. He has a bald head just like Marc!" The office was excited because they thought this baby boy was a perfect fit for us. We were told he was five months old but the information in our hands showed he was born in January 2014 and appeared to be eight or nine months old with a little hair on his head. I showed Marc the picture and he said, "Really? That is our baby?" I told him something wasn't right. Something had happened. The Holy Spirit was tapping me on the shoulder to let me know I needed to push this. This was not the right referral. When we received that first referral and I showed him the picture he basically said, "Okay fine, then this is it." There was that tap on the shoulder again. *"Tegra, get on the phone now, call the agency and tell them how you are feeling."* I called and told them something was wrong, that they told me the child they referred had a bald head and was five months old but the picture of the child they sent looked older. The young lady I spoke with asked to call me right back and when she did, she apologized profusely. "I don't know how this happened. We sent you the wrong referral." To myself I thanked God I pressed. She continued, "I'm emailing you the correct information now!" As soon as I saw his picture I said, "This is our child!" Once again, I'm thankful I'm in tune with God's Spirit. I fell in love with Yakob the very first time I laid eyes on his picture. He was instantly our son! Marc shares the same sentiment. It was all so right, there was an instant bond.

The agency in Ethiopia does not want you to see the child until it's time to pick him up. Marc and I didn't really care what the rules were. We were compelled to go and see our son and were off to Ethiopia again to see him, hold him, and love on him. Ahmed had already seen him because we gave him a picture after everything was approved and asked him to go and check on him. He not only went to see him but took pictures and sent them to us. We began getting pictures of him every week.

When Yakob was first presented to us he was crying and a bit fussy, but it only took thirty minutes for him to calm down and rest in our presence. It was difficult for us to leave him there and not bring him home with us that month. There was paperwork that still needed processing, so we needed to rest in patience. Marc encouraged me, "Tegra, I'm certain Yakob will be with us by Christmas." I just kept looking at him, something in the back of my mind wasn't sure it would happen. My senses were correct. It was going to take a few more months before we could bring our little cargo home. We had to go back to Ethiopia for a court date in March, and then on April 10th, 2015, on my fiftieth birthday, we finally left for Ethiopia to get our son! This was by far the best birthday gift I've ever received!

When we brought Yakob home, my mom was there to greet us, and he instantly went to her as if he knew her in the spirit. Every single person that Yakob met, he seemed to recognize. There was a spiritual connection there. Even when we landed in D.C. and experienced a layover before flying into Los Angeles, Marc's sister Christy was there with her husband Adrian and three kids, Skye, Blaze, and Hayes. Yakob instantly went to all of them, each one individually! We had his baby dedication in June of that year and almost everyone that ever prayed for him during that season was there. He went to every single person like he knew them in the spirit. It was unbelievable to witness.

For roughly eight years we had many people in our community on this journey with us. They were praying, interceding, and believing with us we would ultimately have a child and become parents, however God wanted it to occur. This was His will from day one.

I was part of a group of eight women who were longing for a child. We prayed every week, and I can say that five out of eight of us became parents. Such a beautiful ending. God truly blessed us!

Chapter Eight

It Is Still Your Baby

MUSIC PLAYS A ROLE IN EVERY ASPECT OF MY life, not just because I was in the music business for over a decade, but because I enjoy quality music, particularly worship music. It really does something for my soul.

A dear friend of mine called me during the time I was going through my health challenges. I shared what was going on and told her I was scheduled to check into the detox center in San Diego. She said, "Okay Tegra, you need to have the best praise and worship music!" I told her I already had a lot of music. I could sense her eyebrow raise through the phone when she asked if I knew who Martha Munizzi was. I didn't know. She said, "Okay, I am sending you her CD and you must take it with you." Okay, fine. But by the time I was leaving for Lemon Grove the CD had not arrived. It arrived later in the afternoon after I'd departed LA. I told Marc that my friend said I must have that CD and I needed him to bring it to me. He said, "Well babe, I won't be there until probably week after next." I said, "Oh no, I need the CD and you have to drive down and bring it to me because she's saying I need to hear this music while I'm here." He said, "Okay fine. I'll bring you the mail and you can have the CD." You know what? My friend was spot on. Martha Munizzi and her CD was and remains unbelievable.

Her entire album lifted my soul. I played it over and over again, all throughout the day for three weeks. Praise and worship music is great particularly when it's ministering to you from a biblical perspective, from the word of God. That is how it was for me, and that's what this artist has woven throughout many of her songs on this particular album. I soaked in it. I've always enjoyed praise and worship but in this particular season of my life I was taken to another level.

The morning Marc was driving me to Cedars-Sinai to have the partial hysterectomy, I once again played Martha Munizzi's music. I was sitting in the passenger seat next to Marc and before I knew it, I was on the floor with my hands raised high praising the Lord and sobbing out of control. Don't even ask me how I was able to position myself comfortably in such a tight space, my husband has a two-seater Mercedes Benz! Marc said he just looked at me. Every time I hear Martha's music, I'm instantly transported back to where I was during one of the most difficult seasons of my life. He shared the story later with Yakob, "I looked at Mom and wanted to say, 'Get up, are you crazy? What is going on with you?' But I couldn't say anything. I just looked at your mom and said, 'Okay she's doing what she needs to do right now. Alright.'"

My friend was exactly right as to why I needed that CD. It

made my time at the detox center significantly deeper with the Lord. Meeting that woman who told me her abortion was nailed on the cross was the first time I was clearly able to see my own sin. Music being woven into my time there was extraordinary.

Even though I went through counseling on my journey to healing, I realized I had never named my child until I went through my own healing process during bible study. A few weeks after my meeting with Bishop Ulmer when I presented him with the vision the Lord had given me for No Longer Bound, I signed up for a thirteen-week group bible study for women who were dealing with pain from abortion. I felt like I needed to participate, since we were planning to start offering the program the following year but had not seen the group model. Toward the end of the thirteen weeks, we had a memorial service for our aborted children. We also wrote a letter to the Lord regarding the abortion or wrote a letter to our child. We were also required, if we could, to name the baby. I thought, *"Oh my gosh, why didn't I ever think about the importance of naming not just my aborted child but my miscarried child?"*

A few days ago, I pulled up a letter I wrote to the Lord. In November of 2009 I was praying and asking the Lord to help me name my child. I did a significant amount of research and within a couple of hours He gave me the name. The name is Or'el Doron. The origin is Hebrew and means "the light of God." Doron which is also Hebrew means "present, gift, offering." I opened up this letter to the Lord starting with scripture. It reads:

For I am convinced that neither your life, neither angels nor demons, neither the present nor the future, nor any powers, neither height nor depth nor anything else in all creation will be able to separate us from the love of God that is in Christ Jesus our Lord. (Romans 8:38-39, NIV)

You knew me before the foundations of the world were formed, before I was formed in my mother's womb, that I would make a selfish decision to murder my innocent unborn child, Or'el Doron. Before the foundation of the world was formed, before Or'el Doron was formed in my womb, you knew my child would never reside on earth. I am thankful and grateful that you are an Omnipresent God. You were in the room with me when the abortion procedure happened. I know I broke your heart and you grieved over my sin. My own desire was more important than your desire, and I chose to do everything which went against your word. Don't grieve God, don't break his heart, his Holy Spirit moving and breathing in you. It's the most intimate part of your life, making you fit for himself, don't take such a gift for granted. (Ephesians 4:30, MSG)

In January 2009, one day following our first embryo transfer into our surrogate, for the first time in my Christian Life I found myself grieving over doubting you. The grief took me into a place I had never felt before. At this moment today, as I look back on that day in January, when my heart was broken and I grieved over doubting your power, I experienced what you must have experienced as you watched what was happening in that abortion room many years ago. I vividly remember a few days following my abortion I was in my bed. It was still morning and your voice spoke to me. "You have not really repented. Get up now." I moved out of the bed and walked into the living room, fell to my knees on the side of the couch, cried out to you, and really pleaded for your forgiveness toward me for murdering my child. I know the Holy Spirit carried me from the bed to the couch and placed me at the feet of Jesus. It was during this time with you that I received your forgiveness. Little did I know, I would not realize that I never forgave myself or others until many years later.

I never thought about naming my own unborn child until today. I love Hebrew names and when I saw the name Or'el Doron and looked up the meaning of "Light of God," I knew this would be the perfect first name. When I came across the name Doron and I looked up its meaning, it meant "present, gift, offering." I knew this would be the perfect middle name. I do not know the gender of my child who is with you in heaven, therefore I wanted to choose a name appropriate for a boy or girl. I'm looking forward to you surprising me in heaven. I've never thanked you for caring for my child, Lord. For taking care of Or'el Doron. I know Or'el is experiencing the greatest love, because there's no greater love than Heavenly love. From the way things look now, I will probably never be able to experience what it feels like on earth to look into the eyes of a child who has my DNA. I will have this experience in heaven, and I am tremendously thrilled.

I purchased seeds today and I plan to create a small herb garden in honor of Or'el Doron with the following herbs: basil, dill, lavender, mint, sage, and thyme. A garden represents life, sustenance, healing, peace, sanctuary, faith, and power. All of which you have given me. I know the smell of the earth will stimulate my senses and will continually bring to my remembrance how you turned my darkness into light. I am humbled by your love for me, and I never want to forget EPHESIANS 3:17- 19. *May Christ through your faith actually dwell, settle down, abide, make a permanent home in your heart. May you be rooted deep in love and founded securely on love, that you may have the power and be strong to apprehend and grasp with all the saints, God's devoted people, the experience of that love. What is the breadth and length and height and depth of it, that you may really come to know practically through experience for yourself, the love of Christ, which far surpasses mere knowledge without experience, that you may be filled through all your being, until all the fullness of God may have the richest measure of the divine presence and become a body wholly filled and flooded with God himself.*

One thing I never got to say to Or'el is, "God loves you and so do I. You are the apple of his eye and the apple of my eye." One thing I was never able to do with Or'el was teach my child biblical principles, morals, and values. One thing I have always been afraid of is—not afraid but more so aware—that there are consequences to sin, and what possibly happened to my body as a result of having an abortion. It hurts the most when I think of how I allowed my flesh to fall prey to Satan's tricks. He didn't pay one cent to live in my mind, heart, or soul yet I opened the door and allowed him to live rent-free, instead of giving full control to Christ, who paid the cost to live in my entire being. One thing I will always regret is murdering my baby.

When I see Or'el in heaven, I want to grab my child and give my baby the tightest biggest squeeze imaginable, and then swing him/her around and around in a circle. After we stop laughing, I will tell him/her how much I love and missed them, how sorry I am for following my own selfish desires in murdering them. Please forgive me for my cruelty, Or'el. I want to study Or'el's face and see a reflection of myself. Satan tried to harm me mentally, physically, and spiritually, but you meant it for good to accomplish what's now done. Thank you for turning my mess into ministry all for your glory. Lord, I am amazed by you and how you love me. How wide, how deep, how great is your love for me.

YOUR DAUGHTER TEGRA, NOVEMBER 3RD, 2009.

Or'el has identity now. When I wrote the letter, I didn't know the baby's gender, but over the course of a few years, the Lord did reveal to me that Or'el is a girl and it's great because the name could be for a boy or for a girl. I was in bed one day, I can't remember if it happened in that moment or in a dream, but He showed me this little girl, if I had to guess her age, she was four or five years old, a shade or two lighter than me. She wore a part in the middle of her head with two thick ponytails, and she was smiling. I knew when I woke up that it was my baby girl. The vision brought me such comfort and peace. The Lord showed me her image.

I want my letter to help others write their letters. It will help them to begin, possibly for the first time, to think about naming their child or their children. To give the child a name of significance and not rush through trying to come up with a name, but to sit, meditate, pray, and ask God what the name of their child is, because he already knows. Ask the Lord, "Father what is the name of my child? What is the significance in his/her name?" I think during this time of reflection and healing, every piece of the process is important, and I don't want them to miss what God is trying to do. Sit and be still without any interruptions.

When I was writing the letter on November 3rd, I wrote "*Lord, I'm amazed by you how you love me, how wide, how deep, how great is your love for me.*" I was listening to a song called Amazed by Desperation Band over and over again. The lyrics are, "Lord I'm amazed by you, how you love me, how wide, how deep is your love for me." The word of God was flowing throughout that song. How wide, how deep is your love for me, in spite of what I've done, your love is still wide and deep and great! Again, I harkened back to my meeting with the woman at the detox center in San Diego. She was right, my abortion was nailed to that cross when Jesus died, because He loved me that much! Everything God does is out of His great love for us. He took me from shame and secrecy to get me ready for ministry. This had to be done before I could cross over into this next phase. No Longer Bound launched in January of 2010. This was the bookmark, the missing piece that was necessary for me to step into the next chapter of my life. How could I have gone into ministry without doing this? Without giving identity to my child? Identity is important.

Almost everyone who has gone through No Longer Bound's program named their child. If they don't name their child, they say "My Baby," because we give out Certificates of Life for each child. Some parents can't choose a name at that moment, and we respect that. Picking a name is like adding flesh to bone and can be too painful if they are not ready to go deeper into the healing process.

When we complete with them on Saturday night it is often pretty late as we are preparing them for the memorial service on Sunday afternoon. Before they are released to go to their rooms, they've actually sat for a good thirty minutes to figure out what they want to name their children. A few will get up at 2:00 a.m. to send a text message or change the name because the Holy Spirit has dealt with them in the wee hours of the morning. We put all the names on the memorial program, and they understand the seriousness in naming their children. The same year Rahel passed, Marc and

I were leading the group alongside team members, we also became retreat participants. In October 2013, we decided to place Rahel's name on the program to honor her by lighting a candle with everyone else. I told Marc the night before that we never named our miscarried child, and he was surprised as well. He said, "I am going to name our miscarried child Hannah. It was a girl." That was exceptional to me. For the first time, we memorialized Hannah. It took many years, but it was still wonderful lighting a candle for Hannah as her mother and father.

Chapter Nine

Daddy Find Me
~
Apostle Paul

HAPPY BIRTHDAY TO ME! THE PHONE RANG, AND when I answered, I was happy to hear my grandfather's voice on the other end of the line. He was calling with all the birthday wishes and accolades one might expect to receive on their birthday. I had just turned twelve years old. When we came to the end of our conversation he asked to speak to my mother. For some reason, I didn't hang up the phone and kept listening. The next thing I hear is my grandfather asking my mom, "Gwen, when was the last time you talked to Paul? Do you ever talk to him?" My mom was obviously disturbed by the questions, and I was a little thrown off as well. She answered, "No Daddy, why would you ask me that?" I could tell she was trying to move him away from his questions. I had taken a gifted test at school one day and as the counselor was going over my records, he asked me to tell him about my father, Paul Hearns. I was puzzled. In so many words I told him he was wrong and that my father's name was Willie Smith. He replied, "No, it says here Paul Hearns." I filed it away and just said, "Okay, I'll talk to my mother and get clarity today. What you have is obviously a mistake." When I did bring it up to my mom later that day, she totally dismissed me and said, "Oh honey, yeah, I'll find out. I'll talk to them and find out what happened." A month or so later my grandfather called, and I heard the name "Paul Hearns" again. I was curious of course but decided to let it go.

My birthday was in April and then Mother's Day was on the horizon in May. That was a little less than a month after having heard the conversation on the phone between my mom and grandfather. On Mother's Day, we were at my grandmother's house who was actually divorced from my grandfather. My mother was there with her kids and one of her siblings. My Aunt Sharon, who I am very close to, was also there. She is like a second mom to me. That day she called me over to her and said, "Tegra, I want to tell you something, come with me into the back room." Why did Aunt Sharon need to take me into the back room to talk, I wondered? All I was doing was hanging out in the living room at my nana's house. When I went into the back room, she started off by saying, "I love you, and you know how very special you are to me." Well, this was nothing new as she always said these kinds of things to me, but she went on with a concerned look on her face. "What I'm about to tell you is for your protection, just in case Willie tried to do anything wrong to you." Then here she comes with the blow of blows, "Willie is not your father." I was aghast but held it together as long as I could. I knew it, I knew it, I knew it! What she said confirmed everything for me. What I heard on the phone between my mom and grandfather, and the information from the counselor at school now made perfect sense. God stepped in and said, enough of this!

I felt like I had cotton in my throat and couldn't believe what I was hearing because first and foremost, I should have been hearing it from my mother. I don't recall Aunt Sharon telling me not to say anything. She just wanted to tell me for my own safety and protection. A day or two later, my mom made dinner for me and my siblings. I was sitting at the dinner table with them and just started crying. My other siblings were looking at me like, "Tegra, what's the matter? Are you okay?" That's when I let the cat out of the bag, "Aunt Sharon told me Daddy is not my father." They couldn't believe it! Everything stopped in that moment. Mom came into the room and asked us what was wrong. It was either my brother or my sister directly under me that blurted out, "Aunt Sharon said Daddy is not Tegra's daddy." Mommy just froze. I looked at her, feeling alone, betrayed, and discounted because I didn't understand how my own mother could take the chance of someone else breaking the news to me. For some reason she just couldn't do it. Ten minutes later, Willie walked in and sensed the unusual atmosphere. He noticed all of the commotion going on and asked, "What's happening here? What is going on?" The tension in the air was thick, and in unison everyone shouted in disharmony, "Aunt Sharon told Tegra you are not her daddy!" At that point I could care less what he thought or had to say, because even in the midst of my tears, sitting at that table I was glad it was confirmed Willie was not my biological father. I was elated in that regard but very sad my mother did not tell me.

Though I am healed from all of this, there remains a

stain. I can see the kitchen clearly. I even remember where I was seated and that I couldn't finish eating my food. I went into the bedroom that I shared with my sister Charron and my mom came in and sat down on my bed. She put her arm around me and said, "Honey, I was actually going to tell you before you started junior high school." I asked why she didn't tell me years before and she just said, "We're going to talk about this later. We will talk about it." I felt abandoned and dismissed. I wanted to talk about it then, while it was happening in real time, but she probably had to talk to my stepfather and I'm certain she called my Aunt Sharon. My aunt probably told her it was time for me to know and once again, she wanted to protect me.

A day or two later, my mom and I went to grab a bite to eat. The bulk of our conversation happened in the car. That is where she began to tell me the story about my real father, Paul Hearns. She was young, only twenty-two years old at the time she got pregnant and had me. She said, "Your father said he wanted to marry me, but he also wanted me to go to Michigan with him because that is where he is from and where most of his family lives. He wanted me to meet them, but when I got there, I found him to be a rolling stone. He would leave me in the apartment all night by myself." I was probably about six months old. She told me that my grandfather on my father's side said she should not have come there to live with his son, and if he had known she was coming he would have told her to stay in California. Paul's father knew the type of man my father was. He was six or seven years older than my mother. She would ask him what he was doing, but he never had an explanation. My mother was absolutely alone and scared, so she picked up the phone and called her father.

She asked him to send her a ticket back home, which he did immediately. She got on the plane with me in her arms and never looked back.

I can only imagine how afraid my mother was, living in a state she had never even visited. She didn't know anyone but my father. Yes, she had met a few of his relatives and remembered his brother Roger being extremely kind to her. Even he told her she shouldn't have come to Michigan. So she had warnings from the family, but what I couldn't understand is why she didn't have access to any of his family members. They weren't listed and he obviously was not trying to find me. All he had to do was call 411 or look in the White Pages. I asked my mother if any of his family knew I even existed. Well, his brother Roger and his father knew, but they didn't care to find me either. In that moment it became clear that nobody was looking for me. There is a slight possibility they didn't have my mom's information, but that's how I would have to sum it up.

However, I must say it is nothing short of a blessing that I didn't have a relationship with him from the age of twelve until the time I found him. Knowing the type of man he was, I would have had far too many issues. The number one issue would have been the spirit of abandonment. Of course, since then I had matured and grown into a beautiful relationship with the Lord. I know He is truly my Father and He shielded and protected me from what my father could have done to me emotionally. I just thank God I didn't experience rejection at the hands of Paul Hearns. Every year up until the time I actually found him, I longed to know and see him. I wanted to see if I looked like him. Also, I couldn't understand how my mom didn't have any pictures of my father, not one photo. I believe she said she got rid of everything when she moved back to Los Angeles. That symbolized closing the chapter on that part of her life. She closed the door and threw away the key.

Meeting My Father

At thirty-four years old, I was working at Maverick as V.P. of Sales for the entire country. I had to travel to Dearborn, Michigan for a meeting with Borders Books and Music at their corporate office. A light bulb flashed, and I thought, "*Maybe I can find my father. I'm traveling to Michigan and that's where he is from apparently.*" I remember being so excited! An entertainment icon has a brother named Michael who is from Michigan, and we were friends. I thought he might have family in law enforcement who could do some research to help me find my father. I talked to him and he said, "Yeah, I have family in law enforcement!" He turned me on to someone named Samuel, who did all the security for Maverick Recording Company. Michael said Samuel would help me find my father. I talked to Samuel and he said, "Just give me what you have." I told him, "I don't have a lot of information. I only have his name and his age. He was twenty-nine years old at the time I was born. That's all I have. I don't have his social security number, driver's license, nothing." He said, "Okay, no problem, let me get back to you." I kid you not, in a matter of fifteen minutes, twenty max, he said, "Tegra, this is what I pulled up." There were pages and pages of information. He said, "I believe your father is in this area. There's an address, but there's no phone number. Here's the address, these are the cars registered to that address, and these are the neighboring homes within a certain mile radius of where your father is." I was floored and became stoic because I was in complete shock. I couldn't believe what was placed before me. There was a possibility I was going to see my father for the first time since being born.

Samuel asked, "When are you leaving for your trip?" I said, "I'm going to leave Monday or Tuesday." He said, "Well go ahead and send your father a note to this address overnight and see if he responds." I said, "Okay." I was nervous typing the letter to him. I do remember saying something like, "Hi Paul. My name is Tegra Hearns Little, and I know you know the name because you named me." I told him I was working for a record company and was scheduled for a business trip in Michigan the following week. If he got the letter in time, I asked him to call me because I would love to talk with him and see him. I overnighted the letter on Thursday and he got it on Friday. Joyce, my assistant at Maverick who was just the best, came into my office and said, "Tegra, your father is on the phone." Everybody knew what I was doing in the office. They knew Samuel had possibly found him and that I was sending out this letter. I said, "What?" She said, "He's on the phone." I had given him my cell number, my office, and home number, every single number on me. Joyce continued, "He's on the phone, you want me to close the door?" I said, "Yeah, close the door."

I'm there at my desk, and these feelings are coming back up. I took a few deep breaths before I picked up the receiver. Man, was I ever nervous. "Hello?" He answered, "Tegra, well, this is your deadbeat dad." That's exactly what he said. He continued, "I am so sorry, but when I read your letter, I was so glad to get it." Then he tried it. "Yeah, I've been trying to find you..." I immediately cut that off and said, "No you haven't been trying to find me." That was the first horrible thing he said. I countered, "You are lying. You haven't been trying to find me. I was too easy to find." I let him talk, and he told me I had some siblings in Los Angeles. I asked if he had their contact information and he said he didn't, but he knew their names. He asked, "Do you know Yolanda and Trent?" I said, "Oh my gosh, but you don't know where they are?" Now this really triggered me. When I had my conversation with my mother that day in the car, she told me, "Tegra, your father had some other children and I remember the mother of those children. She and your dad got into a bad fight one night. I remember because he came over to my house before we left to go to Michigan, and his face was all scratched up. That woman did that to him." In hindsight, she was probably upset when he told her he was leaving Los Angeles and moving back to Michigan. She probably had a fit and fought with him. I remember my mom saying, "You have some other siblings, but I don't know who they are, where they are, or anything."

When he told me about them on the phone, it took me back. The fact he didn't know how to reach those kids affected me at my core. I thought he wasn't at all a responsible man. He then began asking what I did at the record company, and informed me that I had another brother, Kwan, who was also in music. He had graduated from Berklee College of Music in Boston and of course, I knew all about that school. Berklee is known as a great institution with notable alumni. He said that brother of mine was very talented, and that he had actually married his mother, but they divorced. My father gave me his phone number. Besides one other brother, that was the only person he was in contact with out of that sibling group. I connected with my newly acquired brother immediately after getting off the phone with Paul. I also told him I would be traveling to Michigan and where I would be staying, all the details, and he said he wanted to see me. I said okay, I would be there for three days and could meet him on the last day of the conference I would be attending. I told him he could meet me at the hotel. He was really looking forward to seeing me, and I must admit I felt the same way. Our conversation went well. After we hung up, I opened the door to my office to find everyone at Maverick in my area. They were all like, "What happened? What happened?!" It felt like a scene out of a sitcom, like *Friends* or *The Office*.

I couldn't wait to share the news and called Marc and my mom right away. I told everybody at the office what was happening, that I would finally be able to see my biological father. They were all happy and excited for me. All of this was happening at such a good time in my life because I did not need a dime from him. I didn't need or want anything from him but to see him. He also told me I had cousins, an aunt named Jean in Michigan, and an aunt named Yvonne who lived in the Bay area. A whole new family was out there for me to meet and get to know!

I arrived in Michigan, checked into a hotel, and did what I needed to do businesswise before calling my father to let him know I was available in the afternoon. I asked him to come to my hotel room and gave him all the information. When he knocked on the door, my heart sped up and I completely froze. I felt like I was standing in quicksand and turned stoic from shock. My father was standing on the other side of my hotel room door and in seconds, after three decades, I was going to see him face to face! What was probably only seconds felt like a couple of minutes before I could even open the door. The moment of truth had come. I finally opened the door and there he was, my father, standing right in front of me. He came into the room and we hugged, after which he just stood there and stared at me. He just kept staring and said, "I have to look at you. My God, you are gorgeous." "Thank you," I replied. "No, you look so much like your mother, Tegra!" I just couldn't believe I was now in a hotel room meeting my biological father in the flesh!

He had on overalls like he had been in the woods and so much hair on his face with this thick sort of salt-and-pepper grey beard. He wore a baseball cap and I remember it had the word Union on it. He was affiliated with Ford Motor Company. There were hiking boots on his feet, the kind you wear in the woods. As I gave him the once-over I thought, *"Why is my father looking like a werewolf?"* Did he not think he should have shaved, gotten a haircut, and cleaned up with some nicer clothes? He's an outdoorsy, blue collar sort of working man. Hey, what can I say? He said, "I want to take you to your Aunt Jean's. I told her you were coming and they're waiting for you at her house. Your cousins are there." Wow, was I surprised! He asked if I was interested in going, I said yes, and we were off! While we were driving to Aunt Jean's house he was talking about my different aunts and cousins, and about his brother who lived in Seattle at the time. He has since passed away. Way out of left field I blurted out, "Do you ever shave?" I can't even believe I said it and laugh about it now. He looked at me as if to say, *"Did I just hear her say that?"* I said it again, "Yeah, do you shave? Do you ever shave?" He said, "Yes I do Tegra. I just came from work and didn't have time to get myself together, but yeah I shave and yes I get haircuts." I threw it away and said, "Okay, I was just wondering." He laughed and chuckled at me.

We arrived at my Aunt Jean's house which is located in a beautiful part of Detroit in a well-appointed home. I walked in the door and it seemed as though I was looking right at myself when I met my Aunt Jean. I look so much like her. She is a tiny little woman, very classy, and loves the Lord. I remember my father sarcastically describing her as very religious but hey, that was right down my alley! She was a very Spirit-filled, loving woman. My father was far away from God and just didn't have it in him to connect with her spiritually. I met her daughter, Cousin Almitra, and her husband at the time. I believe she had six or seven kids. She was a homeschool mom and I was blown away by that. My Aunt Jean was an educator who may have been retired or getting ready to retire. There were many other relatives there, too many to mention, but we had such a great time getting to know each other. Everyone was taking pictures and laughing. Aunt Jean made a great dinner, and we enjoyed a wonderful evening. When my father was taking me back to the hotel, I told him I would love for him to visit me in California. He was definitely up for the trip!

When I returned home, I shared the experience with my mom, and she started crying over the phone. This was the second time she confessed my father was the only man she ever really loved. Surprisingly she then said, "Give me his information, I want to talk to him." To be honest I was hesitant. My dad and I needed time to build our relationship first. I said no but told her I would ask to see how he felt. She understood and said, "No problem Tegra, I'm so glad you found your father. Hopefully you both will develop a relationship." I answered, "Well, we'll see." Dad was fine with her having his contact information and looked forward to their conversing. They developed their own relationship and remained in contact with each other. During Christmas he came to Los Angeles for my annual tree trimming party with friends and some family. Marc's mom also visited with us. I introduced him to all of our guests, "You know it doesn't matter what happened in the past, what matters now is how we're going to move forward. I'm blessed to have found my father." He met everyone and they clapped and thanked him for coming.

Paul was a jazz aficionado and loved music. During his first visit, we took him to a jazz club and to LACMA, where jazz is played on Friday or Saturday nights. We went to three or four different jazz spots and he really had a good time. Dad enjoyed smoking cigars, as did Marc. When Marc's dad visited once, the three of them stole away to this little cigar bar in Pasadena and had a great time bonding.

My dad and I talked often throughout the first year. In the spring of the following year, I traveled back to Michigan and returned again in the fall for another business trip. He asked, "Why don't I just come there to the hotel and we'll have dinner there?" I told him it was a fine idea. Let me tell you, my father arrived looking like Marvin Gaye, as clean as I don't know what! I said, "Oh my gosh, you look amazing!" He said, "Tegra, this is how I look. You saw me before when I had just gotten off work, but this is how I am if I'm going out. You talked about me so bad I couldn't disappoint you again." He was clean, had on a nice black suit with his little African scarf. His face was clean-shaven, and his hair was nicely cut. I was stunned! He even brought me a gift. It was a beautiful necklace with a heart on it. He just wanted to give me something, which I thought was nice and very kind.

I was thirty-four years old when I first met my father twenty-one years ago. He mentioned when he retired from Ford, that he wanted to come back to California to live. I told him okay. He told my mom the same thing.

Fast forward to five years or so after we met for the first time. My father ended up getting diagnosed with prostate cancer. My mother went to Michigan to help him recuperate back to health. She flew there for his surgery and while he convalesced at home for a week or so, she was there right alongside him to help. I asked my mom, "Why?" She said, "Well, your father doesn't really have anybody else to help him. I told him if he wanted me to come, I would assist." My mother has a very kind heart. But I still couldn't believe it. She was still in love with him from way back in the day, which I couldn't understand particularly since a tremendous amount of time had passed. Unfortunately, a few months later, after his surgery, he became a different person. He stopped returning my phone calls and it got to the point where I wrote him a letter to see if he would respond. He didn't respond to my letter; he wasn't even calling my mom back and it just became strange. I remembered asking Kwan if he had talked to him, but he couldn't give me a definitive answer either. He said, "Tegra, I don't know, but this is what he does. This is totally his MO. He stays around for a while and then he just reverts back to abandoning people." He was a big-time rolling stone. I chalked it up to, "this is what my father does, and I don't know if our relationship is going any further." When my father came to visit me the first time, I told him what Willie did to me. He put his head down and reached his arm out, took my hand and said, "I'm so sorry. I'm so sorry I wasn't there for you to protect you from what you experienced. I'm sorry." I thanked him and was glad I was able to share my misfortune with him. I also told him what Douglas the lifeguard did to me and again he was completely sorry.

There was a time when Marc and I were attempting our last experience with surrogacy, while experiencing a tough season financially. Money was really tight, so I wrote my father a letter to let him know about our financial hardship and asked if he could help Marc and I out in any way. I had never asked him for anything prior. He ended up overnighting me a check. But yet he wasn't calling me back. He didn't call to talk to me, he just sent the check, which was a shock. I was extremely appreciative of his kindness and sent him a thank-you note. I think what was going on with my father was due to the prostate cancer, it somehow messed with his manliness, if you will. I think it threw him a curveball and he wasn't ready to handle it. He knew that he was never going to be the same again sexually because he had even told my mom. My mom said, "You know, your father is saying he wants to come back to Los Angeles so we can be together." I said, "Mom, you don't want to go down that road. Wake up and stop living in a fantasy." To this day I still believe he was leading her on.

I was finally able to get him on the phone after calling him for three years straight. He was just not being responsible and calling back, but one day he answered the phone and said, "Oh hi baby, how are you?" I pulled the phone away from me, looked at it quizzically, then said, "What do you mean? I've left you so many messages, and you can't call me back. What's going on with you?" He threw out a bunch of weak excuses. He said he was raising hunting dogs and they are like his kids. I said, "Your attention is all on your dogs, Paul." He said, well yeah, I love my dogs and I go hunting with this person and that person and so on and so on. I said, "I don't understand why you didn't call me back." He said, "Well, I haven't received any of your messages." I said, "You know what Paul, stop!" I never hesitated to tell him how I felt. I told him to just stop it because I knew he had received my messages and chose not to call me back for whatever reason and it was okay. I was just glad to hear his voice. He told me he was feeling a lot better and eating lots of organic food. "Yeah, you should see me. I look really great!" It was a very shallow conversation, and I was frustrated.

In 2014, I called to let him know we would be adopting Yakob. He said, "Oh wow, well I can't wait to meet my new grandson!" I said, "Wonderful!", that he could come to us or we would travel to him. He never followed up on anything. I received a call from my Aunt Jean that December to let me know my dad had a urinary tract infection and was in early stages of dementia. She said he had been moved to an elderly care facility for rehabilitation and gave me the number of a lady who was caring for him. She was a long-time personal friend, the daughter of one of his dear friends. I felt fine about it and called her. His caregiver told me everything and I felt it necessary to come and see him. She agreed. I asked her about his bills and how they were getting paid. She had been taking care of everything and because I didn't know her, at first I felt uneasy about her handling his financial business. I had never heard of this person before from my father, at least I didn't think I had. I came out to see him in December.

He was no longer living in the senior care facility but was back home living by himself. His caregiver would come over to check on him about three days a week. When Marc and I got to him, he once again looked like a werewolf. His toes looked really bad, like no one had cared for them. He looked terrible and unkempt. My father was diabetic, and I saw far too many packages of cookies on the side of the dresser next to his bed. I was very troubled by what I witnessed and believed if he stayed there, he was going to die. He needed better care. All of this was happening in 2014. Marc looked at me and basically said, "Well, whatever you want to do Tegra, we will just have to figure it out." Marc's ninety-seven-year-old great-aunt was living with us at the time, and had the entire bottom level to herself with her own caregiver. We were trying to figure out what we should do, so we decided to get rid of a gym we had set up in the house and arranged that space for my father. All of this was going on in the midst of us not really knowing when we were going to leave for Ethiopia. We were in this whirlwind, and everything was moving way too fast. My father ended up getting another urinary tract infection and had to have surgery then return to the senior care facility. At this point we knew a firm decision had to be made.

I went back to see about my father and found he was still dealing with early stages of dementia, so he wasn't really remembering a lot of things. I said, "Paul, here is what we need to do. I need to be power of attorney over all of your affairs because I need to know what's going on and I need to protect you." He said, "Of course Tegra, you are my daughter. Whatever you think is best, let's do it." Great! In my mind the caregiver had access to all of his accounts and everything. She could have been stealing him blind for all I knew, but he said, "She's been so good and caring for me. I know her mother, I know her sisters, I know her family. I've known them for thirty years. She's honest." I said, "Well, we will find out." I took him to the bank so he could get her name off of everything. The branch manager took me into another room and said, "Tegra, these are all of your father's accounts. She could have wiped him out but hasn't done anything wrong." I reviewed everything and it was evident the bills were being paid. I was relieved to see she was a woman of integrity. That brought tremendous peace and gratitude for her honesty.

I'll never forget when my father was in the senior care facility and having to put his signature on everything. I brought an attorney to do the proper paperwork he also needed to sign. He was acting like he didn't want to sign it. I had to get a notary to come to the hospital and she was asking him certain questions my father did not know the answers to. She said, "Mister Hearns, who's the president?" He looked at her, gave her a tricky little side-eye and said, "Come on, you know I know who the president is." She said, "Why don't you go ahead and tell me, then?" and he couldn't tell her it was Barack Obama. He didn't know Michelle Obama's name and so she said, "We have a problem here, Tegra." I said, "No, let's get my Aunt Jean on the phone, she will talk to him." I asked Jean to talk with him and she assured him that I only wanted to give him the best care possible. She told him to do the right thing and come to California with me and Marc and to sign the paperwork. Thanks to Aunt Jean, he said yes and signed everything. The notary was comfortable and signed off on it as well.

We had to put my father in long-term care at the center where he was until we could figure out what we were going to do. Marc's Aunt Sunita passed away at the age of ninety-nine in June, so I immediately went to Michigan and packed my father's things. Aunt Sunita's caregiver flew to Michigan with me to help get my father in and out of the wheelchair. We brought him back to Los Angeles and set him up in Aunt Sunita's old space. It worked out perfectly! He had a caregiver and a great geriatric doctor at Huntington Memorial. He was thriving even though his mind was diminishing. He would often ask about his mother, Roger, and people who had died but his mind was lucid in the morning. We played jazz music for him and he was truly happy.

Dad's Damascus Road

One morning I went downstairs as I always did to check on him and make sure he was doing okay. This was in June 2016. I said, "Hey, you're up!" It was probably 6:00 a.m. and I noticed he had one of the No Longer Bound brochures on his dresser next to the bed. He was a voracious reader, so he was constantly reading early in the morning. I said, "Hey Paul, were you looking through the brochure?" and he answered, "Yeah, I was reading it." I said, "You know, have I ever talked to you about No Longer Bound?" He said, "No, I don't think you have." He was so sharp and lucid, so I began to talk to him about the ministry and I also shared with him about my abortion. I said, "Paul, I'm so sorry because I killed your grandchild. You have a grandchild you will hopefully see in heaven." He was just sitting there on the bed. I asked him if he was okay because he had his head down. His eyes were filled with tears, I said, "What is the matter Paul? Do you have abortion in your background?" He said, "I used to perform abortions." He blew me away with that confession. I was shocked!

I quickly pressed the recording button on my cell phone. My father was not a doctor. "What are you talking about?" He began to share a secret he had buried deep down inside for years and years, "I used to perform abortions. When I was around nineteen years old. I was an orderly at a hospital in Michigan. This white doctor used to walk around the hospital showing off wads of cash, and he asked me if I wanted to make that kind of money too. Of course, I said yes. This doctor taught me how to do abortions and I started to do them illegally, outside of the hospital with this woman and we made tons of money. I was wearing the finest clothes and driving nice cars but eventually I had to stop. I couldn't do them any longer and told the woman I was done." The tears began streaming down his cheeks and I said, "Oh Paul, I am so sorry that you went through that. But we serve a God of forgiveness. He forgave me for having my abortion and I know he will also forgive you for performing them. What I want to find out from you right now is if you died today do you know where you would spend eternity?" My dad grew up a Seventh-day Adventist, so I figured he possibly accepted Christ when he was a kid, but I didn't know if he currently had a relationship with Him. He said, "Yes." I said, "So you've accepted Christ as your Lord and Savior?" He answered, "Yes I have." I said, "Oh, okay fine." But he needed to hear that God forgave him. He was so broken until he heard what I said. I could tell it resonated with him. The words I spoke were a healing balm in that moment. I laid hands on him and prayed for my father for the first time. It was extraordinary.

After I left the room, I just praised the Lord. I never would have known had he not been living in my house and read the brochure next to his bed. He started performing abortions at nineteen and I had my abortion at nineteen. Only God! It is so clear my father had the spirit of abortion on him. He had eight kids by eight different women and aborted those relationships. He aborted relationships with pretty much every one of his kids! But that's how much God loved my father. He loved that man and for the end to come full circle where I would be the one out of all of the siblings to care for and watch over him to the very end of his life was beyond what I could have ever imagined.

He took his last breath at Glendale Adventist Hospital. I got there five to ten minutes after he had taken his last breath. I was able to sit there in the room. Marc and Yakob met me there as we were in separate cars. I just threw on some clothes when the hospital called because they told me I should come immediately, but I got there after he died. He looked so peaceful. Marc and I really weren't sure when they arrived if Yakob should see his papa, but we actually left it up to him and he said he wanted to see him. He came in the room and touched him. It was a sacred time for the three of us. My father wanted to be cremated so we had a special cremation service for him. He died January 19th, 2020, just days away from his eighty-fourth birthday.

It's a beautiful love story, different but a love story none the less. I'll never forget the first time I had to bathe my father. It was an honor to serve him in that way. I bathed him, oiled him, and washed his hair. He was so appreciative of everything I did for him. Caregiving is a blessing. It's one of the hardest jobs, especially when dementia is involved. I was blessed to serve my father in the last four years of his life.

Chapter Ten

Purpose in the Pain

I AM IN A PERPETUAL STATE OF PEACE AND QUITE content. I say this because of where I am with the Lord. Residing in my heart is a peace that surpasses all understanding. Even in chaos or whatever may be going on in my life, I have peace. God has never left nor forsaken me and continues to provide every step of the way. My needs are always met and here I find comfort.

This is an exciting time in my life. Parenting is extremely wonderful! My son, Yakob, stretches me. Every time I am pulled to what seems beyond my breaking point, or my patience hits a wall and I can't take one more thing, I come to a screeching halt because I hear the Lord saying, *"Okay Tegra, you need to hold the mirror up right now."* I let go of the need to control and find myself reciting PSALM 139:23-24, *"Search me God and know my heart; test me and know my anxious thoughts. See if there is any offensive way in me and lead me in the way everlasting."* I have learned to apologize without delay to my son.

Yakob is one of the instruments God uses to make me a better Christian. It's amazing to be tested in this way.

I've heard many testimonies and stories from women, saved and unsaved. Raising children is certainly challenging to say the least. Believe me, I am a witness! Kids can drive you to the edge, but I find calm when I step outside of myself, take a look at my behavior, and own it. Instantly I pull my son close and apologize. Switching to distance learning due to COVID-19 stretched me. There were days when I wanted to escape to a remote mountainous area to just scream. I recall the day when we hit a bump in the road. Yakob was not focusing on the various tasks I was asking him to handle. I started screaming then stopped and told myself, *"Tegra, you need to calm down."* I thought Yakob had misplaced something that belonged to me, but I later found it. With sorrow and humility, I said, "Oh my goodness Yakob, Mommy just found it, come here let me give you a hug, sit on my lap." He was leery at first and replied, "No, mom." I beckoned him again with, "No, come here." Finally, Yakob walked over to me with his head down. I sat him on my lap and said, "You know what? Mommy is so imperfect, and I make mistakes. Every time I make a mistake, don't I tell you I made one? Don't I also apologize and say that I am sorry?" He said, "Yes, you do." Then he gave me the biggest hug, as if nothing ever happened. Isn't that just like our Heavenly Father? He forgives us and places it all in the Sea of Forgetfulness.

This style of parenting is good for me and fastens me to stability. My relationship with Marc and our working together in No Longer Bound is also good. September 2021 grants us twenty-seven years of marriage. We've been together for a total of thirty-five years. I can honestly say if we hadn't put

God first, we would be divorced. Thank God we are evenly yoked. A three-prong cord is not easily broken! Thank God for Jesus, the Holy Spirit, and the willingness of my husband to adhere to God's principles. He has his own relationship with Christ. If he didn't lean on Christ or have a loving relationship with Him, our lives would be severely different. We are two imperfect people in a marriage led by a perfect God. In times of crisis, we did the work it takes to keep us together. Also, in every hurdle and struggle along the way, I often return to a vivid memory of my wedding day. I was sequestered in a room prior to entering the space that leads to the aisle. There I am, standing in my gown and I begin to see the heavens open with angels singing over me. I know this sounds surreal, but it happened! The atmosphere was heavenly, and I heard the angels singing so beautifully. This memory is as vivid today as the day the Holy Spirit picked me up from my bed and placed me at the feet of Jesus. This vision was my confirmation from God letting me know He was pleased that Marc and I were becoming one.

Throwing in the towel is easy to do. You have to press through pain and trials. Every marriage has them. The question is, are we up to doing the real work? Because it does take work, hard work, but there is a purpose in the pain. There was purpose in the pain of my abortion. There was purpose in the pain of me trying to become a mother. There was purpose in the pain of finding my father. Wasn't there a purpose in the pain of my molestation? Wasn't there purpose in the pain of my marriage? Purpose is bountiful! *"Lord it is okay. Stretch me because I know that what you are trying to do here is bigger than me and Marc!"* It's all about God and what He wants to do! To this day, I still become very emotional when I think about how He brought me through my cancer battle and I never once asked why. *"Why did you do this to me? Why did this happen to me?"* I never once asked why because I understand purpose. I knew God was going to get the glory. And He did!

Life is not easy. We live in a fallen world and our journeys will never be easy. Even if you are a multi-millionaire, life is not easy! There is pain in this world, pain and tribulation. It motivates us and is the tool God uses to sharpen, mold, and shape us so we can live in eternity! The people we love most sometimes hurt us on the deepest levels. We need to avail ourselves to love and understand hurt is part of the process. We can deal with whatever comes our way. I'm willing to see, to be tested, and taken through the fire as long as God is at the helm.

There are two scriptures I constantly lean on when faced with adversity:

> *When you pass through the waters, I will be with you; and when you pass through the rivers, they will not sweep over you. When you walk through the fire, you will not be burned; the flames will not set you ablaze.*
>
> ISAIAH 43:2, NIV

> *No temptation has overtaken you except what is common to mankind. And God is faithful; he will not let you be tempted beyond what you can bear. But when you are tempted, he will also provide a way out so that you can endure it.*
>
> 1 CORINTHIANS 10:13, NIV

If I believe God's Word, I must trust the process. This is my personal declaration.

In the area of ministry, I know there's a lot more on the horizon for No Longer Bound. As founder and president, I desire more partnerships in churches throughout the United States and globally. Ultimately my big dream for No Longer Bound is to have its own retreat center. We won't have to partner with certain retreat centers and adhere to their schedules or restrictions. God has shown me how it looks. He gave me the vision and I know it will come to pass! I'm not anxious, I rest in what I know he has shown me. No Longer Bound belongs to God and when the hearts of those within this organization are pure for His Kingdom, He will provide. We are His hands on earth to accomplish His mission.

I have a deep passion for women to receive their healing, but I also carry the same passion for men! Our men are also hurting. Unfortunately, many organizations don't reach out to them. The Lord has given me a great gift of discernment to know when someone has abortion in their background. I sense it automatically. I can share my testimony, but sometimes I know when I have to step back and bring in a man as a "closer," if you will.

Years ago, the Holy Spirit spoke to my heart, *"As men begin to show up, they will become the front line for No Longer Bound. When they are emboldened to unashamedly step forward and say, 'I am so sorry. I am so sorry I took you to the abortion clinic, dropped you off and left you there. I'm so sorry I was never there to hold you or to tell you let's do this together.' The women will see them and say, 'I am signing up for NLB because I see our men being healed!'"*

When our male leadership speak and minister to these men, the groundwork is laid, and they will join.

Minister David Williams sums this up perfectly in his Men and Abortion Network blog:

> *The fullness of the gospel message is compromised when our leaders fail to address this issue in their own lives. It communicates that "my position, image and ego are more important than letting Christ take full possession of my life..." especially those areas that are most shrouded in secrecy and shame.*
>
> *I told this young man that through some unexpected circumstances and people that God showed me that a key source of my being stuck had to do with the abortion of my child. In 2013, twenty-two years after the abortion and sixteen years of being a Christian, I went through a post-abortion Bible Study that God used to bring healing to me that I did not even know that I needed. And five years later, my relationship with God and my family, though not perfect, is so much healthier, richer and vibrant.*
>
> *After I shared, this young man thanked me, and then his demeanor changed. He rolled up his sleeves and said, "now I can tell you what is really going on in my life." He alluded to the fact that because I was a Pastor that there was no way that he could share with me his story. But once I shared with him, it gave him the safe place to finally be honest with someone.*
>
> WILLIAMS, 2018, PAR. 7-8

We all need to pray for men to get their healing. It is clear that the enemy of our souls' intent is to castrate and keep them isolated, so they never walk in their God-given purpose.

The Church

"I would rather go to God with an abortion than to the church with an unplanned pregnancy." This is not a simple phrase, but a heartbreaking chorus sung by women who are ashamed to share their secret with the church. The place that should beckon them with open arms and hold them tight as they fight through the pain. Why haven't we taken our cues from Jesus who protected the prostitute on the verge of being stoned to death? Or the Samaritan woman he openly engaged with? God help us! My prayer is that the body of Christ will elevate itself and fully embrace everyone with mercy and compassion. People desire and need a safe place to open their hearts and say, "This is who I am. I need help without judgment or condemnation, without being shamed. I want to be honest about all my weaknesses and ugliness. Please accept me the way I am. Otherwise, I can return to the world and they will accept me. I really do want to be here in the church, in the body of Christ, where I've been told I will be accepted, but will I really? Can I trust you?" Until that time comes, No Longer Bound is the safe haven and our arms are open wide.

We look forward to implementing five-day healing retreats for men and women who have been physically abused and sexually molested.

Some of our leaders have experienced the benefits of this specific ministry. We attended a retreat in Houston, TX with a similar mission and I loved it. There were different breakout groups which stayed together throughout the course of the retreat. Two men with amazing testimonies were in my breakout group. They were comfortable and transparent in ways I've not experienced as they spoke about their molestation. They felt safe in the environment, didn't care who was in the room, and were open and strong in their sharing. Both men were married but one was going through divorce. All of them had children. They wanted their freedom and went all the way! The ministry has to be replicated everywhere, and No Longer Bound will help set the example.

Molestation happens more often than not, and the percentages are astounding. Out of the 400+ people that have gone through No Longer Bound; I would estimate 98% of them have molestation in their background. How can we not reach out to those who have been molested? We must!

If I Can, You Can

God is truly the author of my story. He delivered me and I was ready to do the work. If there is abortion, a miscarriage, abuse, or whatever is challenging your life, I want you to say, "If God can do it for Tegra, I know he can do it for me. I'm finally ready to surrender."

You must be willing to confess. If you have abortion in your background, confess that sin to God and he will forgive your sin. Reach out to No Longer Bound and get your healing. There is help available even if you don't live in California. Join a bible study for abortion, miscarriage, or physical/sexual abuse recovery. Now is the time! Lastly, remember, God didn't heal you just for you. His mission for us is never just about us. It is always about Him and how we can be His hands here on earth. Now is your time to help others!

> *"For I know the plans I have for you," declares the Lord, "plans to prosper you and not to harm you, plans to give you hope and a future."*
>
> Jeremiah 29:11 NKJV

References

Rowland, Katherine. "Microchimerism: How Pregnancy Changes the Mother's Very DNA – Katherine Rowland: Aeon Essays." Aeon. Aeon, January 11, 2018. https://aeon.co/essays/microchimerism-how-pregnancy-changes-the-mothers-very-dna.

Lehr, Jennifer. "Shame: You Are Only As Sick As Your Secrets." LoveAndLifeToolBox, June 22, 2018. https://loveandlifetoolbox.com/shame-you-are-only-as-sick-as-your-secrets/.

Williams, David. "Abortion and the Church." Men and Abortion. Men and Abortion Network, May 1, 2018. https://www.menandabortion.net/index.php/2018/05/01/abortion-and-the-church/.

For Speaking Engagements, Book Signings, Appearances, and Interviews...

Contact

nlbunborn@gmail.com
info@nolongerboundministry.org

833.NLBOUND (833.652.6863)

https://www.nolongerboundministry.org

facebook.com/no.l.bound

@nolonger_bound

Made in the USA
Monee, IL
19 April 2021